# the minimalist garden

# the minimalist garden

## Christopher Bradley-Hole

THE MONACELLI PRESS

First published in the United States of America in 1999 by

The Monacelli Press, Inc.

10 East 92nd Street, New York, New York 10128.

Library of Congress Cataloging-in-Publication Data

Bradley-Hole, Christopher.

The minimalist garden / Christopher Bradley-Hole.

p.  cm.

ISBN 1-58093-055-7

1. Gardening. 2. Minimal art. I. Title.

SB453.B689  1999

712'.6—dc21          99-32815

Printed and bound in Hong Kong

# contents

# Introduction

There is a new form of garden-making that perfectly expresses the mood of our times. It is contemporary and yet its ideas are rooted in the traditions of the past. It is in tune with technology and makes the best use of natural materials. It is exciting (and can be breathtaking), and yet it exudes tranquillity and relaxation. It can be simple, but can also hide a treasure trove of subtlety and complexity and be deeply symbolic. It can form the perfect, muted, background for planting, but it can also be colourful and make dramatic use of space and light. It is a wonderful setting for a wide range of plants from around the world which can be grown in the most naturalistic and ecological ways. It is equally relevant to Western and Eastern cultures and traditions. It is the minimalist garden.

"Less is more". In 1959 the celebrated German architect Ludwig Mies van der Rohe used these three words to describe one of his current American projects. His statement was reported in the New York *Herald Tribune*. It must have seemed a curious concept at the time, although it did perfectly capture the essence of the minimalist design philosophy. One expression was more eloquent than two. But did Mies mean that you just had to remove an idea from a design to improve it? Not quite. For Mies was urging something more than restraint. He was also saying that when you reduce the ideas, then each idea has to be better than it was before. And it is only if the ideas are truly outstanding that it will be possible to distil them to create something that is unique and special.

▼ Underlying the breathtaking simplicity of Jigsaw, a clothing shop in London, designed by John Pawson, is a rigorous design philosophy involving the complex interplay of spaces and proportions.

▶ In Shaker furniture, form results from function, but the style is characterized by carefully judged proportions which speak simply for themselves. No further ornamentation is required.

Today minimalism is a term that is in wide circulation, and most people have some concept of what it implies. Purity, smooth, clean lines, geometric shapes, no clutter, muted colour, and tranquillity would be the sort of images that the concept conjures up. But such descriptive terms would most probably be inspired by photographs they have seen because few people today own, or even have visited, a truly minimalist house or garden.

The minimalist style has an attraction that reaches right across the spectrum of peoples' backgrounds and experiences. It has a modern image but it is not just the young who share in its delight. For its calmness and modesty have its roots in the traditions of different ages and cultures. Minimalism owes some of its inspiration to the meditative religions of Far Eastern cultures, to the pure geometric proportions favoured by the architects of the Italian Renaissance, and to the simplicity of the Shaker movement in America. There is something essentially right about minimalism, something which corresponds to the emotions and feeling of well-being and energy.

But it is also a break with the past. It can symbolize a clarity, a fresh approach, a clearing away of the clutter of earlier times. It can be something starkly modern, exhilarating and refreshing. It can symbolize a new beginning.

How does minimalism relate to the development of garden design? If we look at the development of gardens we can see that minimalism is the continuation of a thread that runs right through Western and Eastern garden-making. The oriental gardens of China and Japan have, in general, used a very limited range of plants. Instead their design has concentrated on the symbolic elements, such as rocks and water, and how they could be used as a distillation of nature. They are places of contemplation. Zen Buddhism inspired the 15th-century garden of Ryoan-ji in Kyoto (*above*), and it is outstanding for its disciplined, minimalist depiction of a dry landscape.

In the Western world, gardens were an essential part of the great ages of art and architecture. Some of the Italian Renaissance gardens were as complex and intricate as the villas to which they related. The gardens of the Villa Lante, near Viterbo, for example, stand as a superb architectural composition in their own right. The materials, proportions and hierarchy were a reflection of the quality and thought in the surrounding architecture. This was the time of the enclosed garden, with its patterns on the ground often an abstract version of the house's layout. The gardens were the connection between the villas built on high ground and the spectacular views beyond.

▼ The oriental concept of *ma*, or
the space between objects, can be seen
in Wagamama, a Japanese restaurant in
London, where form and function
are in perfect balance. The clarity
of expression is continued with the
graphic design of the restaurant's name.

wagamama

When this style was translated to England in the 18th century, garden-makers were influenced by other inspirations they had found on the Grand Tour. The romance of the countryside and the paintings of the artist Claude Lorraine lead eventually to the "natural" landscapes of Capability Brown and others as the foil for the grand architectural statements. Just as the architecture had developed as it had moved across countries, so had the style of gardens, and that style, known as the English landscape garden, became influential around the world. There was return to a more formal style in the industrial age of the 19th century, but with the influx of so many new plants and materials from around the world, the style became eclectic, heavily patterned, and disorientated. Restraint was displaced by a horticultural form of showing off, but the connection with the architectural style continued.

Although they were overelaborate, Victorian gardens were still in tune with the ostentation of the architecture they accompanied. The 20th century brought a rash of new styles. In England the elegance of the Edwardian era led to the Arts and Crafts style which set the pattern for the new English garden. This was a formal approach, but

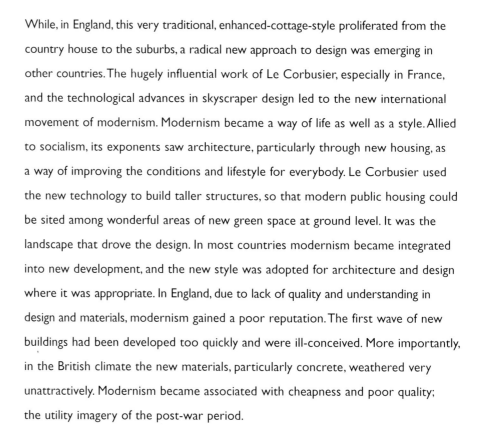

▲ The understated design of this classic Porsche 356 sports car encapsulates in our minds images of speed and engineering without the need for any decorative frills.

▼ The design of this contemporary, Norwegian-made cutlery is minimalist but it still conveys balance, fluidity, and the different purpose of each piece.

scaled down from a classical to a vernacular form, and came to be overlaid with the abundant and tasteful cottage-style planting that was favoured by Gertrude Jekyll. The Edwardian approach led to the making and preservation of hugely popular and influential gardens, including those at Sissinghurst Castle in Kent and Hidcote Manor in the Cotswolds. It was a style which was not threatening or particularly challenging, but it was immediately pleasing and easy on the eye.

While, in England, this very traditional, enhanced-cottage-style proliferated from the country house to the suburbs, a radical new approach to design was emerging in other countries. The hugely influential work of Le Corbusier, especially in France, and the technological advances in skyscraper design led to the new international movement of modernism. Modernism became a way of life as well as a style. Allied to socialism, its exponents saw architecture, particularly through new housing, as a way of improving the conditions and lifestyle for everybody. Le Corbusier used the new technology to build taller structures, so that modern public housing could be sited among wonderful areas of new green space at ground level. It was the landscape that drove the design. In most countries modernism became integrated into new development, and the new style was adopted for architecture and design where it was appropriate. In England, due to lack of quality and understanding in design and materials, modernism gained a poor reputation. The first wave of new buildings had been developed too quickly and were ill-conceived. More importantly, in the British climate the new materials, particularly concrete, weathered very unattractively. Modernism became associated with cheapness and poor quality; the utility imagery of the post-war period.

As the English cognoscenti retreated into a nostalgia for a seemingly gentler time, modernist gardens never had a chance. The English mild climate was ideal for growing the wide range of plants that were newly available, and with its popularity among the middle and upper classes, gardening became associated with good taste. Even so, the 20th century has witnessed the first disconnection between gardens and the associated world. Despite all of the amazing technical developments, the English Edwardian style of gardening is still as prevalent at the end of the 20th century as it was at the beginning.

However, other design elements – architecture, interiors, graphics, product and industrial design – have moved confidently forward and become popular with the general public. There is a thirst for new ideas about design and a wealth of new outlets in which to communicate them. So, it is not surprising that those who are forward looking are also seeking a new approach to garden design that is relevant to the rest of their experiences.

The people who are making the important gardens today are those who are interested in the way the world is developing and are helping to shape its progress. They are educated in history and are concerned with a balanced ecology and sustainability. They see the benefits of technology but they are also in touch with their emotional and artistic sides. They are looking for gardens that will reflect and enhance their experiences in life. Those who are working to their full potential do not want to retreat to a pastiche of the past for their garden environment. They are seeking a new expression which is relaxing as well a stimulating, but most importantly connected and relevant to their experiences and ambitions. The tranquil, modem, energy-creating balanced world of the minimalist garden has arrived.

▶ Sculpture or furniture? The concept that imbued the creation of this chaise longue, made from moulded plastic, could not be simpler, and yet it is expressive way beyond its function.

# the extended home

An example of how the distinction between the inside and outside of a house can be blurred is shown in this house in Mexico City, designed by Manuel Mestre. The space is protected from the weather by concealed glazing, although daylight is still allowed to punctuate the courtyard. Traditional materials are used, but their application is unadorned. The hard finishes would be rugged enough for outside use, but they are also suitable for indoors, as would be the planting of potted cacti.

# Inspirations for the extended home

The immediate garden beside the house has multiple uses and a long history. It can be a place for recreation, for *al fresco* dining, for providing air and outdoor shade, for growing food and/or herbs, or for entertaining friends and family. Indeed, in the 2,000-year-old courtyard gardens of Pompeii, now released from their tombs of volcanic ash, the urban Roman garden was shown to have considered this space as an integral part of the house, and a place for all of these activities.

This intermediate garden also clearly offers a chance of repose and retreat beyond the constricting rooms of the home, perhaps as a place for meditation and contemplation. This aspect has a long tradition in the Orient, where 2,000 years ago in Chinese cities high walls surrounded tiny, secret meditational gardens of rocks and water. In the present pressured and technological age such places are needed more than ever, and outdoor space is now generally regarded as a premium to be enjoyed all year, or for as much of it as local climate allows.

What is particularly exciting about this is that that external spaces can be designed with the same level of precision as is usually applied to interiors: materials such as stone, timber, plasterwork, glass, steel, and even canvas fabrics may be used outside as well as indoors, providing a crisp extension of the home into the garden. Softer interior elements, such as a rug or a carpet, may also have their equivalent outdoors, in the form of a lawn.

In design terms, for new houses, the garden may be mapped out right at the beginning at the same time as the plans of the house are being drawn up. In this way the inside and outside spaces can develop as one unified entity. In the case of older houses, the remodelling of an existing room adjacent to the garden offers an opportunity to link both indoor and outdoor spaces by using common materials; the light and energy of the outdoors can be brought inside by opening up exterior walls, and allowing surfaces to flow from one area to another.

To develop this connection between the inside and outside it is worth designing the interior and exterior so that both spaces include elements of the iconography of the other. So, for example, the boundaries of the garden would be clearly delineated like walls in a room, and kept largely uncluttered and not overdecorated with plants, while the interior could be finished in materials, such as stone, that would survive just as well outside. To complete this union of the spaces, at night the garden space can be lit with pools of artificial light that will draw the eye from the inside to the outside of the house.

▶ Pieter de Hooch's painting *The Courtyard of a House in Delft* (1658) demonstrates that extending the house and its activities into the garden is not a modern concept.

▼ In designing the Farnsworth House in Plano, Illinois (1946), Mies van der Rohe raised the main volume up from the ground on columns, so the house perfectly engages with the garden. The entry platform is at mid-level between the house and garden.

# A bamboo garden

The architect Vladimir Sitta has designed a small walled courtyard on the approach to an Australian house near Balmoral Beach, North Sydney. A high wall screens the garden from the street, but the side walls have been kept low to allow in light. A smooth travertine stone path, raised above the garden areas on either side, leads to the house's entrance. At right angles to the path are rows of the elegant black bamboo, *Phyllostachys nigra*. Its leaves, rising above the walls, identify the garden within when viewed from the street, while the bamboo's slender stems add a sculptural dimension, which is seen from the house's interior.

The bamboo emerges from slots in the paving of stone chippings, and is one of two key design elements. The other is the strips of polished black granite, over which water flows before spilling into a surrounding trough. The granite slabs give the illusion of deep water, while their glossy finish reflects the wiry stems of the bamboo.

The scheme is rhythmic: although light and open, there is a feeling of illusion and mystery, created by the contrast between reflective and muted materials, and by light and shadow.

▶ A raised, stone-clad path slices through the lateral pattern created by the lines of the bamboo, *Phyllostachys nigra*, enhanced by water-covered slabs of black granite.

◀ Near the ground, the bamboo's black canes articulate the space, while above their leaves allow dappled light to filter through.

*Garden plan*

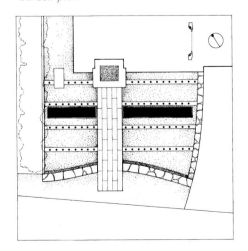

# A central swimming pool

In designing the house for the Sydney-based artist Ken Done, the architect Glen Murcutt worked with the steep slope of the site to create a three-storeyed house constructed around two separate pavilions. Entry to the house is on the upper floor, from which stairs lead down through a skylit picture gallery to the living areas. The lower floor is devoted to the children's rooms; the middle floor is organized around an internal courtyard, with the main living room in the north pavilion on one side, and the parents' bedroom in the south pavilion on the other side.

The courtyard is an excellent example of simple and economic formality, where the swimming pool is the main feature. One of the more interesting parts of the composition is the way in which two voids — that of the pool and the living-room window — interrelate. The swimming pool is flanked to the north and south by two separate terraces, and has been designed so that the water surface is at the same level as the terracotta-tiled terraces and the internal floors. The effect produced is one of space flowing from one area to the next. White walls, the blue of the pool, and light and shadow, echo and reflect the scenes of Sydney Harbour that lies beyond, bringing the glorious views of the bay deep into the house. Yet the space, punctuated by the pool and the single frangipani tree, also has an urban feel that is reminiscent of a small town square in the Mediterranean.

▶ Seen from above, the blue void of the swimming pool echoes the sea beyond, and interconnects the void of the window to the living room. A single mature tree of frangipani casts dappled shade onto the sun-filled terrace.

◀ The pool, which spans the entire width of the terrace, separates one part of the house from the other, but at the same time reflects the surrounding rooms.

# Extending inwards

In hot climates, the idea of the conventional garden is often reversed; in addition to a garden beyond the house and open to the elements and the ravages of heat, there may be an internal space set into the heart of the plan. This internal space or courtyard serves two functions: it brings plants and other natural objects into otherwise enclosed rooms, and it also provides a different type of garden, one that is protected from the elements and is located near the cooler centre of the house. The internal courtyard can thus extend the house internally rather than connect it to the outer landscape.

This idea is very much a part of the modernist approach to design, whereby large glazed walls, both transparent and movable, blur the distinction between the inside and the outside. Although this is a contemporary concept, it can in fact be traced back through historical gardens, and particularly to the architectural principles of the ancient Romans. The traditional Roman house was usually arranged to provide two internal garden spaces: the *atrium* and the *hortus*. The *atrium* was the main, formal courtyard and was open to the sky. It was regarded as the centre of family life, but was also used for public receptions. The *hortus*, set further into the house, was dedicated to *otium*, or free time. It was decorated with statues, fountains and clipped plants, and devoted to growing vegetables.

In modern design, the intention in creating an internal courtyard is to maximize its impact and refreshing qualities by incorporating elements that reflect, in minimized form, the natural world outside. Yet, there is always the temptation, where space is restricted, to overfill the area with too many elements and to bring as much greenery into it as possible. The most successful results, however, are achieved when the designer understands that small garden spaces are an abstraction of nature, rather than a true representation of it.

So, for example, one perfectly formed bamboo set alongside a piece of natural stone is more inspiring than having a clutter of plants and objects. In cases such as this, where the style of the house represents an economical and technological lifestyle, a minimalist approach to the garden space is especially appropriate. As always when the space is small, every item that is included will be looked at very closely; therefore there should be greater emphasis on achieving something of very high quality, especially as the internal courtyard symbolizes the spirit of the house itself.

Light and space are also vital. This is shown in the internal courtyard *(opposite),* designed by Paul Flemming, of a new house in Melbourne, Australia. Situated in an open space in the middle of the building, it has been constructed to let light into the house's heart.

The Japanese flavour of this Australian inner courtyard is created by the black canes of the bamboo, *Phyllostachys nigra*, selected stones, a small pool, and other bamboos used as background planting. Bamboo canes decorate one of the walls.

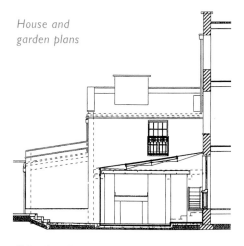

*Side elevation*

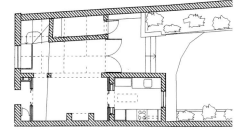

*Aerial plan*

◀ The glazed enclosure creates a new space which brings the garden into the building. The slate floor extends beyond the perimeter glazing into the garden; when the doors are opened the boundary between inside and outside is dissolved.

▶ The glazed roof provides protection to the extended house and frames the view of the garden beyond without screening any of it. The lightness of the supporting structure and its transparent canopy allows visual interplay with the outdoors.

# A garden with a glazed extension

Sanya Polescuk, the architect-owner of this 19th-century house in Hampstead, North London, has extended the ground floor into the garden, thereby creating a space that is an extension of both the house and the garden. A key design element is the lightweight glazed roof supported by a stainless-steel structure that makes a fully enclosed and watertight space when the doors are closed, and unites the interior and exterior when they are open.

Slate flooring has been used to accentuate the flow between the spaces. Internally, the slate has been honed; externally, it has been sanded to make a non-slip surface. The garden store has been treated first with a render and then with a colour pigment added to the final coat to contrast with the house's rear elevation. The garden entrance is arranged so that the enclosed space leads to three steps, which in turn lead up to raised beds overlooking a curved brick terrace with a lawn beyond.

The lower window on the house's rear wall has been converted into a door that gives onto a balcony that is glazed with acid-etched glass – an example of how a design can respect a traditional, existing building and also engage with it to make a contemporary statement.

# An articulated enclosure

One way to achieve a minimalist garden is to separate the boundaries of the garden itself from what is going on within the space. In this type of garden, the boundaries or enclosures need to be seen as a unit, and are usually left uncluttered.

Where the walls have been constructed of different materials, they can be unified by applying surface decoration. Another, less expensive, approach is to install timber fences of the same material all the way around, either decorating them or keeping them as natural timber. More interesting textures and proportions can be achieved by using trellis, which allows light to pass through and gives a three-dimensional textured pattern to the space while still maintaining the ambiguity between open and solid areas. The trellis must have good proportions and is most effective when the grid is small.

Once the boundary fences are unified the internal space can be treated as a separate zone, for example as hard landscaping similar to the floors in the house. The separation of the central space from the perimeter can be further enhanced by an intermediary zone of planting, so that each of the spaces has its own separate purity and function.

◄ From the upper level of John Pawson's house in London's Notting Hill, the garden can be seen as a central activity area of pure proportions. Separating it from the external trellised walls is a narrow zone of planting.

▶ When viewed from the lower level, the stone paving is shown to have been raised away from the ground as a plinth for eating and entertaining. The change of level helps to express its importance in the hierarchy of the design.

# Merging interior and exterior spaces

A key idea in extending the house into the garden is to make use of materials that will work equally well inside and out. This can be achieved by a careful and sympathetic choice of finishes, including fabrics, furnishings, flooring, glass, and plants, that would work just as well in the interior as they do on the adjoining terrace. The overall effect is to blur the edges between internal and external environments. For example, materials such as timber and stone are suitable for both interior and exterior floors and, although they will weather more quickly outside, they will help to tie the design of the two spaces together.

One inspired design idea is to extend a fabric awning over the terrace, carrying the use of soft furnishings — normally found inside — into the terraced area. An overhead awning stretched to a facing wall will filter the light and create shade over an eating area. The fabric, lifting and falling in the breeze, gives movement and life to the terrace. Glass and other reflective materials normally used inside can be used in a similar way. For example, a glass-topped table can act as a substitute for a pool of water in reflecting the sky, while a glass screen can mirror the landscape beyond the roof garden.

A dining area on the terrace can provide the focus for a design. The use of soft cushions on the seating emphasizes the unity of house and garden. The planting can also increase the connection. Tender perennials, such as argyranthemums, which can be grown outside in the summer months, will link with cut flowers indoors; the same material can be used for the pots outside and for vases indoors.

▲ The lightweight composition and reflective qualities of metal containers make them an ideal foil for displaying ornamental grasses.

▶ A calico fabric awning is ideal for bringing the rhythm of sunlight and shade to an external terrace. Soft material, when used outdoors, gives the space enhanced connection with the house's interior.

◀ Oak decking has been used to extend the interior space onto a roof garden, echoing the oak framework of the glazed screen. Planting is simple: a glazed pot of sempervivum, and planters filled with small birch trees that rise out of festuca grasses.

# A frameless conservatory

A garden room allows home owners to experience the pleasures of being in the garden, even when there is intemperate weather, and it is a bonus in cooler climates. Such rooms proliferated in Victorian times in the form of conservatories, and the trend has continued to the present with increasing popularity. The introduction of glass panels and small steel frames during the Industrial Revolution made the conservatory possible, and the dedication of plant hunters who explored the farthest reaches of the world has allowed gardeners to grow, in these rooms, the tender exotic species they brought home. The more recent innovations in construction technology have resulted in the manufacture of glass walls and roofs that are completely frameless. The structure is provided by the glass itself and the silicone-glued joints. This allows the house to be extended in such a way that it appears to reach right out into the garden, so that house and garden seem to occupy one and the same space. The success of this approach depends on carefully linking the materials, building levels and construction methods to give the impression that the house and garden blend seamlessly into one another. When this happens, it shows how modern technology can bring a new creative freedom to house and garden design.

The architect Rick Mather achieves this blend in his brilliant evocation of a garden room for a house in Hampstead, North London. Although the design may at first seem fairly obvious, it is the rigorous coordination of the inner and outer levels of the building – with the outside ground level at the same height as the glazing – that creates the continuity between inside and outside spaces.

◀ The garden space is finished in large beach cobbles at the windowsill height. The frameless glazing allows uninterrupted views of the garden, and at night the myriad reflections from the many light sources create an illusion of mystery.

▶ The construction of the glazed walls and roof is extremely precise. Both the walls and roof are supported by short glass fins, and the structure is held together by a silicone glue. The effect is further enhanced by uplighting set into the windowsills.

# An outside gallery

The connection between the house and garden can be expressed in many different ways, from a formal and positive threshold, or boundary, to the imperceptible flow of one space into another. When designing in a minimalist way, the junctions can be reduced to an absolute minimum. However, reducing the significance of the barrier between the inside and outside does not necessarily make for good design, but it does provide an opportunity to take the design onto a higher plane.

One way of increasing the connection between internal and external spaces is to vary the boundary line for different parts of the construction. So, for example, the external floor surface might continue into the internal space beyond the external windows or doors. Equally, the internal ceiling and wall construction might also continue out into the garden beyond the standard line of the wall. In this way there is continuity between the inside and outside spaces, but also an ambiguity between the two. The success of this approach is largely derived from the simplicity of construction and the detailed design.

In this design for a North London penthouse, the architects Stanton Williams made a wonderful connection between the inside and outside spaces. The internal and external floors can be seen as floating planes interconnecting with each. The internal wooden strip floor in sycamore relates to the external deck in Western red cedar, but the two floors are on different levels, with one step up from the inside to the outside. The architects' solution was to express this clearly, and to have the level of the outside floor enter into the apartment, where it would be seen as a continually overlapping horizontal plane.

The internal ceiling is echoed externally in the fabricated metal *brise-soleil*, which as well as providing shade for the large expanse of glazing, also helps the visual extension of the internal space into the external environment. The solution is subtle, but clear. There is no added decoration, and so the interconnecting geometry is precisely expressed. Restraint, purity, and superbly proportioned components are the dominant features.

The client is a freelance designer. She wanted the space to be articulated in a way that allowed the central living area's open plan to double up as a space where meetings with clients could take place, without the feeling that this was an overtly domestic environment. As both the inner and outer spaces have been kept clear of any added decoration or clutter, they are both perceived as a gallery for her design work. The external deck then becomes a superb opportunity for her to add her decoration of a graded pebble circle, which expresses in the most simple way her intervention in the minimalist garden.

A fine example of the connection between indoors and out: the raised level of the external deck continues past the glazing as an internal step, while the metal *brise-soleil* extends the internal ceiling outdoors.

The minimalist design of the interior of this London penthouse apartment creates a natural gallery for the work of its designer-owner. She has also extended the galley outside the apartment. By placing an inspired sculpture in the form of a graded circle of pebbles, she has captured the external theme.

# An interlinking house and courtyard

This house in Deptford, South-East London, was designed by the architect Mark Guard. It was built within the existing external walls of an old commercial garage, which had been constructed of traditional London stock brick. Within these walls the architect has created a series of modernist, interlinking spaces comprising living areas and courtyard gardens. During the initial design stages, the courtyards developed from the architectural elements, but they soon became the focus around which the house was organized.

Internally, the building is of masonry, steel and concrete construction, with spaces formed by short sections of wall, enclosing but also opening out into other spaces, and creating a light and open environment. An important element of the scheme is provided by the glimpses of different scenes that are viewed from the individual spaces.

The design is a reversal of the traditional arrangement of rooms, with the bedrooms occupying the ground floor and the living areas on the first floor. This arrangement provides views from the upper storey to Greenwich and Thomas Archer's church of St Paul's, Deptford, beyond. From the bedrooms the outlook is to the adjoining courtyard gardens and their defining walls; diagonally, it is to the short, stub walls forming, and allowing glimpses of, the other interior spaces. The interior glazed walls overlooking the courtyard have been organized in such a way that they can be drawn back, in order to complete fully the connection of the house to the garden.

An underlying philosophy of Mark Guard's design is to blur the distinctions between the interior and the exterior of the house. So, for example, the white plaster walls of the interior relate to the white-painted rendering of the courtyard walls, while the raw sealed-concrete floors of the rooms relate to the gravel beyond, which is an abstraction of the internal space. It all creates a free plan in which the garden spaces are integral with the living spaces, and yet are separated by a hierarchy of detailed expression. This subtle division is a tenet of minimalist design, and in this way the garden becomes a modern outside room.

Birch trees (*Betula utilis* var. *jaquemontii*) grow from the limestone chippings of the courtyard, their stems introducing a linear whiteness that enhances the modernist feel. Their gentle foliage allows the light to filter through from above, so that the feeling of openness is maintained. Everywhere there is a sensation of movement and space beyond, particularly in the concrete stairs leading up to the roof terrace at first-floor level, which looks down onto the courtyards at ground-floor level. On the upper level, the leafy foliage of the birch trees screen out the nearby buildings, yet they allow sufficient space for viewing of the different scenes in the distance.

The bedroom opens out into the garden courtyard, while full height glazing connects the two spaces. The slender, white-stemmed birches dramatically emerge through chippings, which are a rough counterpoint to the smooth concrete interior floors.

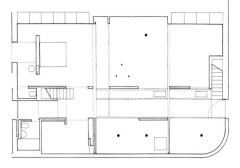

ground floor plan of the house and courtyard

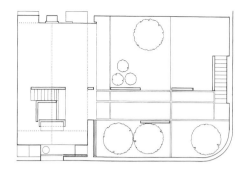

first floor plan of the house and courtyard

The entire design is based around a central pathway leading from the entrance and linking all of the main spaces of the house at ground-floor level. All of the spaces are rectilinear, linking all the main spaces of the house at ground floor level.with a strong feeling of nature pervading each one. The design elements have been kept simple, although each garden space has its own individual character. At the entrance to the courtyard, a long rectangular pool holds aquatic plants and the occasional stepping stone, which is subservient to the main concrete path leading to the front door and the reception areas.

The garden courtyards are the focus of house and are overlooked by all the key spaces; the entrance path, the studio and the main bedroom on the ground floor, and the main living room, kitchen area and the roof terrace on the first floor. This scheme demonstrates how important a garden can be in providing oxygen and energy for all the other spaces.

In a tough, urban environment the architect's ingenuity has created an introspective plan in which the building's external walls are largely unbroken, providing protection from the outside, whereas the mainly light and open internal walls are reduced to an open network of screen walls and openings.

The main axis through the house is by a concrete path and an adjacent pool. It provides a series of experiences via diagonal views past the screen walls to the garden and studio beyond.

# Structural enclosure

For a really successful project, a design scheme must begin with a strong concept. In designing this modernist house in Southwest London for a leading fashion photographer, the architect David Chipperfield introduced a key structural element that would enable him to connect the house to the garden. This was a reinforced concrete beam that spans right across the width of the plot at first-floor level. It is a bold intervention and certainly would not be the obvious solution, but it allows a splendid union between the house and garden. On one side of the house the beam visually encloses the paved external courtyard, and on the other, it frees the external wall from structural demands, making it possible for the wall to be fully glazed. The lateral spine wall can then thrust forward under the beam and out into the garden. The result is an enlivening integration of the internal and external spaces that can be viewed throughout the building.

The floors of the two living spaces are allowed to carry through into the garden on their different levels, which increases the dynamic quality of the design. With such a strong design concept of interlocking spaces, it would only be appropriate for the garden to be treated in an equally bold and simple expression. The planting includes a grove of white-stemmed birch trees (*Betula utilis* var. *jacquemontii*) that beautifully reflect the whiteness of the concrete structure of the building.

This project is a wonderful example of the second wave of modernist architecture and garden design to have been introduced into England. The use of concrete to form the structure allows the creation of interlocking spaces, which would not have been possible using a standard load-bearing construction. The result is a superb feeling of freedom and lightness, which is made possible by this heavyweight construction.

Silhouetted at dusk, the geometric structure of the house contrasts with the soft pools of light in the interior.

▼ A large concrete arch spans the full width of the site. It frees the glazed corner of the living room, completes the visual enclosure of the external terrace, and frames views of the garden beyond.

◄ Multi-stemmed birch trees, with their peeling white bark, echo the pale cream and grey patina of the concrete structures of the house, and at the same time add another texture.

► From above, the garden spaces are seen to be interlinked with the house. A pool lined with paddle stones seems part-house, part-garden, while the grass and birch tree plantings contrasts with the decking.

# courtyard gardens

The courtyard approach to the new
rear elevation of this house in Bayswater,
West London, is a superb composition
of simple elements. To the left a newly
planted stilt hedge complements the
boundary wall, whereas to the right an
uplit, curved wall opens out the new
façade and leads to the solitary purple-
leaved plum tree. Compacted gravel
provides a rough-textured contrast
to the smoothness of the walls.

# Inspirations for courtyard gardens

Throughout the history of garden design, the courtyard garden has been a recurring and important theme. The ancient Persian paradise garden was a fertile enclosure of abundant water, fruit trees, and flowers, in marked contrast to the parched desert beyond its walls. The patio gardens of southern Spain demonstrated an Islamic influence, with one of the finest examples being the gardens of the Alhambra Palace and Generalife, near Granada. In ancient Roman houses there was often an *atrium* – a bright, rectangular space within the house, but open to the sky, making a cool circulation space, and often ornamented with a central fishpond or fountain. The garden beyond was another open courtyard, generally surrounded by a shaded, colonnaded walkway. The apothecaries' gardens and cloisters of medieval monasteries continued the courtyard garden's ancient tradition, and with the rediscovery of classical design during the Italian Renaissance the courtyard continued to thrive, especially in the form of a *giardino segreto*, or secret garden, walled and hidden away from general view. As all of these examples show, courtyard garden's introspective spaces, offered a sense of protection and refuge from the world outside, as well as a place of peace. Inspired by gardens in hot climates, they provided shade protection from hot sunshine and, perhaps, the cooling sounds of moving water.

Contemporary courtyard gardens have much in common with their ancient antecedents. Tranquillity is introduced by keeping the choice of paving and walling materials very simple and unified. Plain-coloured walls, unadorned with plants, will provide minimum

▶ A rectangle of lawn takes on a special importance when it is enclosed by buildings, as in this quadrangle at Magdalen College, Oxford.

◀ The Mexican architect, Luis Barragan (1902–88) has been hugely influential in minimalist design. One project especially, his design for the San Cristobal Stables in the north of Mexico City, encapsulates the essence of his concepts for pure, interconnecting spaces defined by a framework of brightly coloured walls, punctuated by light and water.

distraction and therefore increase the sense of calm; a single tree, perhaps a carob or fig, may be introduced to cast further shade in the hot climate courtyard; in cooler regions it may be desirable to keep the space as open as possible, but offer some textural interest by paving with cobblestones, or laying a smooth carpet of grass. Unlike the cottage style of gardening, where the walls are blurred and clothed with climbing plants, the minimalist courtyard celebrates the boundaries by keeping them uncluttered and unplanted. The space is enjoyed for its own sake, although in order to do that, great care must be taken to get the proportions right.

Proportion is crucial in the design of courtyards. In days of antiquity, and again in the Renaissance, the Golden Rectangle and proportions based on the square provided naturally pleasing and harmonious spaces. Modern spaces based on similar geometric rules continue to please the eye; plain walls of pleasing proportions become features in their own right and thus key elements in the successful execution of a design. Common to all these gardens is the celebration of the enclosed space and an undeniable sense of unity.

# Courtyard with trees

The minimalist garden uses few components, thereby allowing the spectator to enjoy the spaces between the elements. In contrast, there has been a tendency recently for plantings to become cluttered – an expression of abundance with one plant growing through another so that it is not clear where one plant begins and another ends. There has also been a bias towards underplanting trees so that flowers provide year-round interest.

With the minimalist approach the plants are treated more reverentially, with single plants displayed as if they were an object in an art gallery. This gives new opportunities to consider plants for what they are, for their individual character and structure. Within a simple space trees can be used like columns in architecture, their stems articulating the ground space but kept open and separate, whereas above head height the foliage can merge. In this way, shadows can be dramatic, both from the clarity of the stems projected onto the ground and from dappled light that filters through the foliage. There is something uplifting and inspiring in the concept of trees emerging from gravel. It is a very uncomplicated expression, evoking memories, say, of a typical village in France in which the local games of *pétanque* or *boules* are played.

The arrangement of trees can set contrasting styles. For example, a single tree has a precious quality, whereas a random grouping of trees suggests relaxed informality. When trees are arranged in formal spaces, such as a circle or an avenue, it is a clear expression of human intervention in an otherwise simple scene. It is always a good discipline for a designer to use as few components as possible. Without the complication of variety in plants and other objects, the designer must manipulate space, proportion and light in order to evoke the moods required.

*Garden plan*

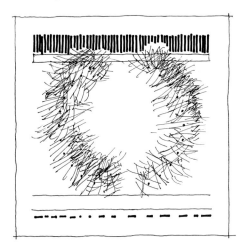

This simple courtyard of stone chippings, designed by Andersson, in Stockholm, Sweden, is based on a square plan, and planted with a circle of willow trees. The trees' shadows help to define the space and their leaves enclose the space at high level.

◀ The circular pattern of sawn logs forming this wall, and the cleverly made bench of tree trunks attached to it, boldly express the designer's central theme of trees and timber.

▼ Timber is virtually the only material used to make the structural elements, but it has been masterfully handled to provide a variety of different textures and even the boundaries of the pool.

# A yellow courtyard

The designer of this stunning courtyard, architect José de Yturbe, demolished his previous home in Mexico, in order to build the house seen here. It was a bold and courageous decision, which is reflected in the design of the new structure.

The courtyard is at the centre of the plan. The overriding impression is one of exhilaration, produced by the use of colour and the quality of the space. In true minimalist fashion, the elements have been reduced to the essentials, so that the perception is one of powerful simplicity. The construction has been kept very simple, using basic materials, such as the rendered blockwork and the concrete steps incised into the wall. The Mexican climate makes the use of such materials extremely successful: in a damper environment they would be subject to stain and discoloration.

A brilliantly executed feature is the diagonal pool that slashes across the courtyard, acting as a moat for the two main rooms of house, the library and the living room. The water in the triangular pool can be likened to a horizontal mirror, retained by the walls of the house on two sides, with a section of pre-rusted steel running diagonally across the courtyard on the other side. The inherent strength of steel has allowed the designer to make use of a thin section to hold back a large quantity of water.

The courtyard walls are massive, and their power is enhanced by the scintillating use of colour, especially the saffron yellow, which contributes a stunning contrast to the blue sky above. A window, highlighted by the pool and coloured walls, has been used dramatically as a frame for a ceremonial bowl from India.

◄ The water in this triangular raised pool is bound on two sides by the house, and on the third side by the courtyard. Like a mirror, it reflects an opening in the wall, which frames a ceremonial Indian bowl, filled with silver *pulqueria* balls.

► The more soberly coloured outdoor stairway becomes an artistic composition in its own right, when seen beside the contrasting strong saffron yellow of the courtyard walls.

Black volcanic stone, found in the vicinity of the house, has been laid as paving on the floor of the courtyard. The one element of luxury is the grid of white marble pebbles, which reduce the scale of the courtyard and introduce a strong geometry. The grid also echoes the grid of the main opening of the library, which is comprised of four massive squares cut into the wall of the house. Complementing the saffron walls of the main house are the muted beige tones of the low wall and the staircase, which leads up to a higher level, where other beige walls have been sliced open to allow an existing tree to punctuate it. The house walls on the upper level are painted a strong terracotta, with a perimeter wall in yellow ochre.

A collection of four olive pots is the single element of decoration in the courtyard, and the eye is directed toward them when descending the stairs. There are no plants in the courtyard itself. However, the walls act as a picture frame for the mature trees beyond the house, which intrude merely as shadows cast upon the walls.

# Walls within walls

The contemporary garden of the Davis Residence on the outskirts of El Paso, Texas, was designed by Martha Schwartz. The clients, Anne and Sam Davis, approached the well-known artist and landscape architect to create a new garden in an old space. The brief was to prepare a design for a walled area between the herbaceous borders and trees of the traditional garden and the garage area.

The available space was approximately 11 x 18m (about 37 x 60ft). The owners wanted something new as a contrast to the traditional garden that lay beyond: a low-maintenance garden with Mexican influences that would include cacti. Another stipulation was that they should not be able to see the older garden from the new one. The result is a series of six introspective garden rooms, built inside exterior walls in a re-interpretation of a Mexican garden, with elements that the designer felt were essential to the theme: formality, geometry, and sparseness.

The walls are the key feature of the new garden, and their painted surfaces reflect their roles in the overall design. The external walls are suffused with sombre colours, whereas the interior walls of the rooms are brilliant blues, pinks, oranges, and reds, with small areas of white. Colour is also used to create a number of individual environments within the overall space. Each room has a different expression. Within the Gold Room, which looks out onto the Rocky Mountains, is a mound of stone chippings that has been conceived as an abstract version of the mountain peaks beyond. Another room, called

*Garden plan*

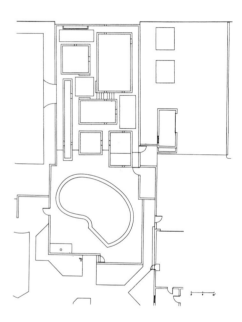

◀ The brilliantly coloured walls of the room interiors are seen through square spyholes which limit the view out. Such tiny rooms and high walls are only practical in climates with reliably strong sunshine that enables enough light for plants to grow.

▶ The designer's three watchwords were formality, geometry, and sparseness, all of which provide the ideal setting to display cacti, making these distinctive plants pieces of sculpture in an art gallery.

◄ The Gold Room features a mound of
stone chippings alluding to the view of the
peaks of the Rocky Mountains, which can
be seen in the distance from within this
particular room.

the Changing Room, contains a mirror and a bed of prickly cacti in front of a bold pink
wall. In the Orange Room, a single tall cactus embedded in coloured chippings makes a
strong vertical statement. Ice-blue glass shards are embedded along the edge of the white,
clean walls of the Bath Room. Beyond the rooms is a pre-existing, kidney-shaped pool
that reflects the darker exterior walls of the rooms. Everywhere the design intention
is to disarm the visitor and introduce an element of surprise.

The high walls of the enclosure create a rectilinear internal space. This is only practical in
climates where the sun is especially strong, and where plants such as cacti are tolerant of
severe conditions. In gentler climates, this degree of enclosure will force plants to grow
straight up in search of light, making it difficult to incorporate plants that need to be
grown in a natural way.

An added interest of this scheme is the way in which Martha Schwartz has updated the
concept of garden design used in the traditional enclosed gardens of the Renaissance,
the hortus conclusus, and the more recent tradition in England of subdividing the garden,
popular during the golden age of Edwardian gardening. In those schemes, green spaces
were often enclosed by hedges to create a series of external rooms. Here, these ideas
have been given their ultimate expression, with masonry rather than hedging creating the
spaces. The feeling is much more of the house being taken out into the garden. This, together
with a sunny climate and deep shadows, allows brilliant colour and minimal but highly
sculptural planting to replace the more verdant, softer expressions of earlier examples.

▼ An aerial view shows how the rooms
relate to each other. At ground level there
is almost the quality of a maze, due to
the sombrely painted exterior walls
and the corridors that run between them.

# Cacti desert garden

Walls are a vital part of the minimalist garden, and can define spaces without necessarily enclosing them. Walls of different heights and thicknesses can give greater emphasis to the spaces to which they relate. They provide protection and a degree of enclosure, suggest movement, and frame views. In certain environments their ability to provide protection is crucial. For example, in creating gardens in a desert, walls will define the areas to be treated as the garden. Within them the effects of climate can be ameliorated, allowing plants to grow and flower for longer periods than they would in the harsher desert habitat beyond. The space can be seen as an art gallery, within which the plants can be viewed as pieces of sculpture. In a desert garden sculptural elements such as the prickly pear *(Opuntia ficus-indica)* and other cacti can be dramatic in their extraordinary shapes and growth patterns.

◄ Wall can determine a garden's structure and also create a dramatic effect. Here, low walls snake through the garden to enclose a raised bed displaying a variety of cacti, verbena and agave species.

▲ In the Sacco garden in Arizona, extraordinary shapes of *Opuntia* and *Fouquieria splendens* are interspersed with long-flowering *Lantana* and shrub *Verbena* to create an almost primeval landscape.

# The garden as a Theatre of Lights

The layout of this small courtyard in an Australian house gives the impression of simplicity. Designed by the architect Vladimir Sitta, it incorporates only a few elements – a terrace, a table and granite slabs – but each one has a reverential quality. And while the composition may appear simple, the courtyard's beautifully proportioned and considered components have been imaginatively treated, transforming it into a fantastic theatrical display.

The design elements have been arranged in horizontal layers: the floor of the main courtyard is composed of crushed green marble chippings, out of which rise four black marble pools – which the designer calls wells – set on thick pieces of sand-blasted glass. Water flows over the surface of black marble from the centre. Fibre-optic lighting cables, sound and misting equipment, and a pump for recycling the water are housed in a concrete chamber below the marble slabs. When light is thrown onto the glass at night, the marble appears to be floating in the pool. Light also passes through holes punctured in the marble and illuminates from below lines of green bamboo set along the sides of each well.

The whole space is enclosed by external walls of terracotta-coloured render. Between the wells and the rest of the courtyard is a threshold – a slab of rough granite – in which the natural fissures have been artificially enlarged to create a piece of sculpture with engaging tactile qualities. The fissures divide the slab into four sections, reflecting the four stages of life from birth to death. They are referred to collectively as The Journey.

*Sketch for the Theatre of Lights garden*

▶ Beneath the slabs are wells containing devices that provide water, fibre optic light shows, misting equipment, and even sound effects. To the side of the slabs, mists can be programmed to float up in clouds which swirl upwards and envelope the garden.

◀ The surface of each black marble slab is always covered by water, which pours out from a ring of holes near the centre, and overflows into the crushed green marble chippings below. The marble slabs act as mirrors, reflecting the stalks of green bamboo overhead.

# A Mexican courtyard

This Mexican courtyard is a composition of light and shade. The rendered walls and the terracotta tiled floor and pot are all from the same warm orange ochre tone, yet their appearance is related entirely to the amount of strong sunlight that falls on their surfaces. The shadows cast by the incised niches and overhanging steps, and the canopy of the single sculptural tree bring interest and mystery to a minimalist concept.

# Inspiration from geometry

Underlying the design of this contemporary garden in Chelsea, London, for *The Daily Telegraph* is a rigorous geometry. Although my inspiration was the pastoral poems of the Roman poet Virgil, instead of giving it an historical appearance, I have created a garden with modernist references. Proportion is the key to the whole composition. This is expressed in the purity of the forms and spaces which make up the design, and the clear route through the site to which other elements relate.

Running virtually the length of the garden is a decking path and raised bed, which are offset to increase the feeling of energy and movement. The path opens up a vista that focuses on a piece of stone, inscribed with lines from Virgil's *Eclogues*. Through the garden, the enclosing walls have been cut away in places to reveal inner panels, finished in marmorina polished plaster in tones of wine red and yellow ochre. All the other major elements of the plan have been designed to precise geometric proportions, mostly related to the square and the "golden rectangle", a system of proportioning used in classical architecture. This has also been the inspiration for the steel and glass pavilion in the centre of the plan. Alongside is a reflecting pool, fed from a stone-lined water staircase over which the water flows before running under a glass bridge to reach the main pool.

At the front of the garden herbs emerge through a courtyard of limestone chippings enclosed by an upstand and low bench of sawn limestone. The vertical planting allows views right through the pavilion to the garden's back wall.

*Garden plan*

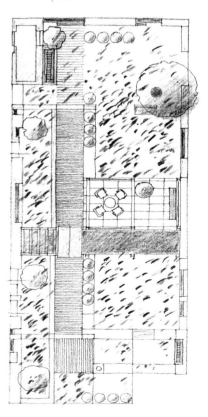

This starkly minimalist plan has been overlaid with relaxed but contemporary planting. The raised bed incorporates several design elements. It encloses the decking path on one side and at one point is crossed by the glass bridge. The central scheme of the planting in the raised bed is to express the idea of a journey through the site; all the plants were chosen to reflect their natural place in the Mediterranean, and in Italy in particular. Throughout there is a swathe of the bearded iris, *Iris pallida* ssp. *pallida*, which is grown as much for its fine foliage as for its wonderful scented blue flowers. This has been interplanted with the deep violet *Allium* 'Purple Sensation', purple-and-white *Acanthus spinosus* – often used as a motif in classical architecture – and herbs such as the blue-flowering rosemary.

Two mature grapevines, *Vitis vinifera*, tower up and over the walls, and at the entrance to the garden is a mature pomegranate, *Punica granatum*. The trunks of the vines and the pomegranate are important for their sculptural quality and maturity as well as for their foliage. The vista of this space terminates on a panel of strong red plaster, which also frames the rectangular slab of inscribed limestone. The vitality of the raised bed, slicing through the entire length of the decking, is enhanced by the buttresses that emerge from the perimeter wall at intervals along the path and frame the views.

Although the original inspiration for the garden was the Roman poet Virgil, the planning is very much in the tradition of Japanese design. The clean lines of the steel, and the Portland stone floor and walls, and the decking, are complemented by the custom-designed planter for the lemon tree, which is fabricated from birch-faced plywood.

◀ The axial path of timber decking and the raised bed's retaining wall shoot through arches to reach a coloured niche on the end wall. The path is crossed by a stairway of water flowing under a glass bridge and emerging into a flat pool beside the pavilion.

▶ The linear raised bed contains plants from the Mediterranean region, including *Iris pallida* spp. *pallida*, alliums, herbs, and standard grapevines. Wall niches feature further quotations from Virgil's poetry.

The walls of the pavilion are of huge, glazed, panels, attached to the structure by stainless steel fittings. The opaque, acid-etched glass has been left clear in places as precisely proportioned horizontal slots through which the view is focussed. By framing small defined areas, it imbues parts of the garden with a reverential quality. The garden is intended to create a series of contrasts between areas where the eye is encouraged to linger on areas of detail, and others where the whole garden is open to provide dynamic views and experiences.

Beyond the pavilion the planting becomes much wilder and richer. This is a reflection of the mature stages of Virgil's life, when he returned to the Italian countryside as a famous and wealthy man. Here, the tall perennial *Thalictrum rochebruneanum* grow like sapling trees out of the meadow-like planting beneath. A thread of purple-leaved plantain leads to a simple stone bench, which is surrounded by cranesbill geraniums in purple tones. Other planting in the long grass includes *Astrantia major* 'Shaggy' and the richly coloured *Aquilegia vulgaris* 'Ruby Port'. In a scene reminiscent of the Roman countryside, the space is overlooked by the stone pine, *Pinus pinea*, and four vertical cypresses.

▼ Sheets of glass, partially acid-etched, are held off from the pavilion's structure and control views. The precise limestone floor and cedar decking is offset by relaxed planting. A custom-made plant case of birch-faced plywood holds a single lemon tree.

▶ Where plants are allowed to take over to provide a rich textural tapestry, it is important to have a strong, underlying structure that holds the garden together. Here it is articulated by the boundary walls, the limestone bench, and carved urn.

# A contemplative courtyard

The external spaces of this new town house in the San Angel district of Mexico City convey a sense of tranquillity. Unadorned walls and paving are used to define the spaces and the colours are muted. Yet the design's simplicity gives a precious quality to each element.

The house contains a superb collection of modern Mexican art, while the high courtyard walls provide protection from the pressures of the city outside. Its designer, the Mexican architect Andrés Casillas, previously collaborated with Luis Barragán on the San Cristobal estate project, and he has brought that project's sense of place to this house. As the layout is inward looking, the design of the courtyard has been given a reverential treatment. The rectilinear plan is an exercise in restraint, while the purity of the proportions imbues it with a spiritual quality.

The design's heart is the reflecting pool, which acts like a moat, separating the house from the outside landscape. Its stillness brings a feeling of calm into the courtyard, while the tranquil water acts as a mirror, reflecting the walls and the planting above. Ingeniously, the terrace has been fused with the pool by taking slabs of local volcanic stone beyond the terrace and out into the water as a series of stepping stones. These appear to be suspended in space above the pool, and look like pieces of sculpture viewed from all sides.

The wall is finished in a render that is pigmented with marble chippings, its beige tone mixing with the muted grey of the stone, and the sunlight and shadows to create a scene of understated harmony. The floating stone path leads the eye away from this restful composition toward the walls at the far end of the pool, which are finished in a contrasting cobalt blue, a colour traditionally used in Mexican houses to ward off evil spirits.

◀ Slabs of dark grey volcanic stone merge from the terrace as stepping stones held above the surface of the still reflecting pool. Its mirror surface gives a mysterious quality to all of the components of the garden.

▶ In keeping with the squared-off geometry of the garden, the sundial is a simple rectangle of carved marble, articulating the progression of the sun through the courtyard during the day.

The courtyard demonstrates how, even when a scheme is reduced to the most minimal, it retains a wonderful quality of surprise. The steps leading up from the courtyard to another level beyond introduce a sense of fascination of not quite knowing what is around the corner. When sunlight floods the steps, this becomes even more enticing.

A single tree emerges out of volcanic stone cubes, used in large sections on the steps, and in smaller units in the more intimate courtyard space. Beneath the tree, a small, simple reflecting pool has a magical quality. Constructed of black metal, it is filled with water, which continually but gently overflows into the narrow trough surrounding it, and produces a sense of calm and abundance. The strong sunlight coming through the tree creates shadows on the wall behind it, and the tree itself is reflected in the pool.

Planting in the courtyard is simple. In addition to the single tree, a pair of mimosa trees with filigree foliage appear to reflect the light of the space. In another area of the courtyard, contemporary abstract art is represented by the work of Xawery Wolski – five terracotta rings held away from the rendered wall. Each ring is exactly the same, and yet has its own individuality, brought to life by the play of sun and shadows.

The opening in the house's wall is seen as a narrow, vertical slot, with darker render beyond. This is another example of how intrigue can be added to a design by giving a hint of what might be beyond the space. With very simple use of materials and planting, the designer has achieved a marvellous control of an enclosed space, leading the eye and mind to the realization that there is something more beyond what is immediately seen.

◄◄ The courtyard is a lesson in simplicity. The stepped design creates a series of vertical panels leading to an intriguing opening. By contrast, the five terracotta rings form a superb horizontal backdrop.

▶ On the lower courtyard the floor is of small cubes of volcanic stone, but the chunky stairway is made of similar stone cut into larger pieces. Although it is difficult to see where the stairway will emerge, it entices the viewer to explore further.

◄ A raised pool fashioned from black volcanic stone is allowed to overflow continuously, thereby creating a surface tension in the water as well as a series of seamless reflections.

# White on white

This cool and symmetrical scheme by
Stephen Woodhams uses a limited range
of colour to enhance its feeling of repose.
A more solid line of neat box *(Buxus
sempervirens)* cubes draws the eye to
a veil of water plunging from a white
wall behind low seating.

# A highly structured house and garden

The brilliant Japanese architect Tadao Ando's Kidosaki House was built 1986–6 in Setagaya, a quiet residential suburb of Tokyo. It was designed for an architect and his wife, and their parents. The building consists of a cube 12m (about 39ft) in length on each side, surrounded by a wall rising to a height of two storeys, which marks the boundary of the site. Within the perimeter walls of the site is a collection of three living units, each with its own private interior space linked to an external space. The courtyards and terraces situated on various levels play a key role in connecting the various living areas, as well as separating them and affording privacy within each unit.

The house is located just off-centre of the site, leaving space to the north and the south. The north space is a courtyard entrance to the house; the south space forms the garden courtyard. The way in which the two courtyards are arranged is in complete contrast to the traditional Western approach to garden design, where planting would be around the perimeter of the space, for example with climbers growing up the walls to reduce the impact of the walls' massive qualities. Here, Tadao Ando has inverted the approach, so the effect of it produces dramatic results. As the high sun invades the courtyards it

*House and garden plan*

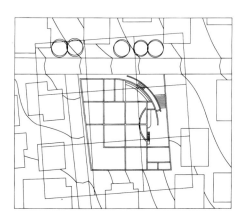

◄ When viewed from above, the dynamic geometry of the house is quite clearly articulated. Within the perimeter walls the square plan of the house is realigned. The two ground level courtyards can be seen infilling diagonally opposite corners.

▲ By keeping planting to the centre of the courtyard, the walls are left bare to receive the changing pattern of shadows from the foliage.

▶▶ At the foot of the steps to the entrance to the house, the multiple stems of the trees, emerging through a ground cover of ivy, provide a sculptural contrast to the precision casting of the reinforced-concrete structure.

produces wonderful moving shadows onto the canvas of the finely honed concrete and the stone floor. In this way the walls are planted in abstract, and yet can still be enjoyed for the magnificence of their structure.

All of the spaces within the perimeter walls have a feeling of both tranquillity and energy, a result of the simple materials used and the way in which the spaces have been planned, with one area leading into another, and with yet another area beyond. In the garden courtyards, birch trees rise out of ground-covering ivy, their peeling trunks reflecting the texture of the surrounding concrete. The slate floors and the grey concrete work together to form the perfect sculpture. Ando is a superb exponent of using structure to invent exhilarating spaces, and here he has managed to achieve a feeling of light and movement within an economical site.

# A central integrated courtyard

At the heart of a new house in Kensington, London, designed by the architect Seth Stein, is an internal courtyard that brings light and energy into the surrounding rooms. Unlike many gardens that provide a contrast to the houses to which they belong, this courtyard is totally integrated. As if to emphasize the importance of the garden, it has been placed in the centre of the plan, and links the main rooms of the house. The garden demonstrates that by the restrained use of natural materials and exquisite proportions, it is possible to create a minimalist garden that is both stimulating and complex, and whose success relies on the way that different parts of the buiding have been expressed in different ways.

The key to simple spaces is thoughful planning in the detail and careful positioning of a limited range of components. Here, square Spanish limestone slabs were used to provide the main area of flooring and a raised bench; they help to organize the space into zones for walking, relaxating and planting. The lawn, which is designed to the proportions of a double square, acts as a contrast to the hard surfaces and a focus for the space; it acts as the equivalent of a rug in an internal room.

However, the internal courtyard is only part of the story of external spaces. The relationship between the internal and external has been explored throughout this house and garden design, which was influenced by the philosophy of design of the traditional

▶ The approach to the house entrance is a composition with underlying meaning. Whereas the pedestrian approach is via a raised timber walkway, vehicles arrive over granite setts, with the house's domain secured by a band of pale beach cobbles.

◀ A gazebo that is cast from fair-faced concrete commands the upper terrace and focuses views beyond. Its circular form sits like a piece of sculpture upon the decking terrace.

that opens to visitors as they move through the garden. Thus the entrance is expressed in a separation of materials and detailing. Vehicles drive over granite setts, whereas pedestrians approach on a raised timber walkway of jarrah railway sleepers reclaimed from the Firth of Forth Bridge. The immediate perimeter of the house is delineated by a separated band of white marble pebbles out of which emerges a single tree and a small fountain.

The theme of light and dark is expressed in the house elevation, where the entrance door is a solid white panel, whereas the living spaces are enclosed with glass panels, acid-etched to defuse the light, but with a clear vision panel set within them. From the entrance approach the visitor is allowed a glimpse of the upper terrace with its unique gazebo, cast on site in fair-faced concrete. The gazebo provides a shelter in which to sit, both encloses and captures the views beyond, and restricts the view at this level. The timber walkway is reintroduced here as a decking terrace of smaller sections of conservation-grade teak; these have been allowed to obtain a silver patina through exposure to the elements. The success of this minimalist design relies on the way that the different parts of the building have been expressed in varying ways to provide fresh experiences.

*Plan showing the courtyard at the heart of the house*

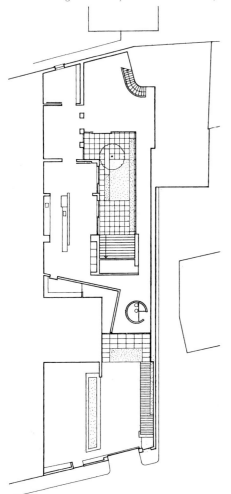

▶ A row of golden oat grass (*Stipa gigantea*), was planted in a channel along the garden's length, separating the pure space of the gallery on the right and the utilitarian kitchen area on the left. It makes the perfect foil for modern architecture.

▶▶ Viewed from the kitchen, the courtyard can be seen as a series of elements which interact with one another. The limestone steps and paving lead to a panel of grass framed by the horizontal lines of the stone bench, decking walkway and line of ornamental grass. The naturalistic character of the grasses brings a feeling of nature into an urban space, while their flowing stature adds valuable height without creating an imposing barrier.

# A Japanese stone courtyard

The design of this courtyard in Urawa City, Saitama prefecture, Japan, appears to be extremely simple, but in fact it is full of underlying complexity. It is overlooked on all four sides by residential units, and the fundamental idea behind the design was to create a central pool that would bring light into the space. Both during the day and at night the focus is the circle of irregularly shaped, sawn and polished stones. They are a reinterpretation of a nebula of glittering stars, a miniature version of the cosmos. Two of the major stones have been sliced in half to respect the main axis that runs through the adjoining buildings.

The similarly irregularly shaped pool is a sea of pebbles. In the middle of this the designer has arranged for a fine mist to rise up among the stones, in imitation of Japan's moist humid climate. At night the design takes on even more dramatic qualities when light glows from the centre of the pool and low beams of light intersect across the courtyard. Overhead lighting throws the trees into silhouette. The whole effect of the garden at night is to give an impression of the vastness of the universe.

The planting is limited to an area of courtyard that receives the best natural light, and here a grove of maples (*Acer pictum*) and bamboos emerge out of sunlit grasses.

Shodo Suzuki, who designed this courtyard, is well known for his use of natural stone in his garden projects. By carefully selecting individual stones he is able to introduce them as uncomplicated sculptures that reflect both nature and design. The massive stones are left with their rough-hewn sides exposed, as they would be found in a quarry, although some of the top surfaces have been sawn and polished to demonstrate that these are not purely a natural feature. Outside the stones, the sea of pebbles is graded to enclose the pool in an irregular shape, so that there is ambiguity about where the pool stops and the beach begins.

*Garden plan*

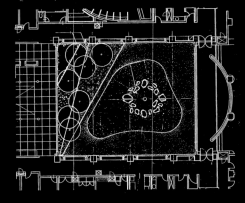

At night the circle of sculpted stones is picked out by sharp blades of laser lighting that intersect across the court. Light also glows from the centre of the pool, providing a focus and dramatically illuminating the misty spray.

# roof gardens and terraces

Cool for cats. This Australian roof garden reveals how materials can be combined to produce a superb contemporary terrace whose modernity is softened by choice container plants. The cantilevered reinforced concrete floor floats above the ground, and turns in on itself to make a seat at the end, while the slender galvanized steel and glass structure adds shelter and overhead definition.

# Inspirations for roof gardens

Roof gardens present a wonderful opportunity for free expression. At ground level, the urge is to relate the garden to the house, its architecture and materials, and the surrounding landscape. On the roof, on the other hand, something with a less earthbound atmosphere can be created. Roof gardens have inherent restrictions deriving from their structure, exposure, and limited access, but with clever manipulation these can be inspiringly explored.

On the ground, trees and adjacent buildings provide privacy, but on the roof there is a feeling of exposure: to the sun, wind and, perhaps, neighbours. Rooftop soil can be three to four degrees warmer than at ground level, accelerating plant growth. Trees are difficult to grow successfully unless the structure can support deep raised beds, so alternative means must be sought to bring about a sense of place and psychological protection.

A permanent overhead framework over part of the terrace will provide control, proportion, and shelter, and a means of supporting screening components and lighting. Ideally, it will be made of metal, perhaps galvanized steel which develops an attractive grey patina. The framework can be designed to span the space between side walls; with chairs and a table underneath, it can form a focus for the whole roof garden.

At roof level, wind speed can be double that on the ground. This affects people's comfort and increases the stress on plants, which need some shelter to prevent damage or distorted growth. Thus plants which grow well in blowy conditions, such as those naturally found in seaside habitats, and those that move with the breeze, such as grasses, make ideal choices.

▲ These terraces are designed to relate more to the wind, sea, sky, and spectacular views than to the landscape below.

▶ The design of this roof terrace at Channel 4's headquarters in Central London extends the internal floor out onto the external terrace. The tapering planks of decking maintain the curved building profile.

◀ In this office building in Norwich, Norfolk, the ground has been transferred to the sky. The lawn and surrounding hedge reflect the sparseness of detail in the building itself.

Landscaping materials also give visual expression to the wind's force. Fabrics such as canvas and sailcloth work well as canopies, awnings and banners. Aluminium yacht masting, combined with rows of high-tensile, stainless-steel wire, may create an open high-tech boundary that enhances the space's the lightness and brightness.

Roof terraces and balconies must be made safe for people as well as plants. Balustrade height is dictated by regulations, but the design can complement and harmonize with the space rather than acting as a visual barrier. Finally, furniture should not be so light that it can be toppled by the wind; small containers should hold a loam-based compost, which is heavy enough to make the pots stable.

Before planning a roof garden, check that there is sufficient structural support to take any additional load. Timber joists are unlikely to be strong enough to bear the extra weight of plants, soil and containers, especially after watering. A modern concrete construction may be suitable, but seek advice from a structural engineer. When the structure's strength is questionable, choose lightweight materials and position all heavy objects (including plants) around the edges, or above load-bearing walls or main beams. This will also be useful during planning as the choice and positioning of plants is crucial to creating a dramatic space.

# A partly enclosed roof terrace

When designing the two-storey Nakayama House in Nara, Japan, the architect Tadao Ando chose to shut out totally the exterior landscape. The result is a house that looks like a shoebox without a lid. By slicing the plan in two, he was able to include a magnificent courtyard on the ground floor that takes up half the site. The rooms on this floor, the dining room and living room, open out onto the courtyard and face a wall opposite. From the courtyard an open staircase leads up to a simple terrace, which is linked directly to a Japanese-style room on the second floor. The terrace takes up half of the top floor space and has been treated as an internal space that only relates to the sky, not to the exterior landscape. Although completely open on one side, it is visually defined by the dynamic concrete beam running the length of the space, giving a feeling of complete enclosure.

A single material, concrete, was used in the construction; it was Ando's intention to purify the character of the space. It relies entirely on the geometry and proportions, which lift it from what could have been a utilitarian space to something quite magical.

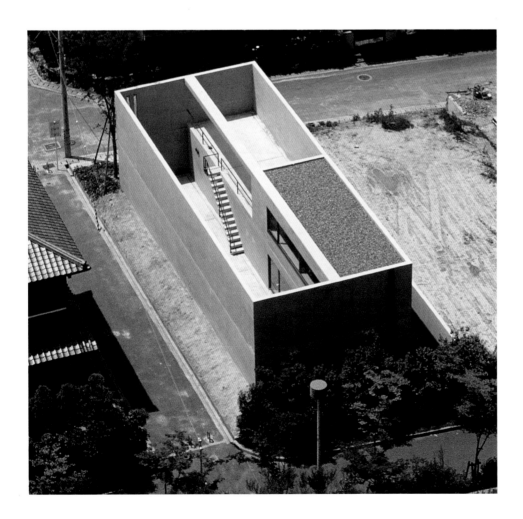

◄ From above it can be clearly seen how the ground-floor courtyard and the roof terrace interlink. The two external spaces are like voids cut out of a solid box.

► The central spine concrete beam bisects the long dimension of the plan and visually encloses the open wall of the roof terrace as it engages with the double-height courtyard to the left.

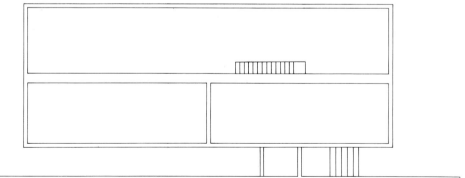

*Top floor plan*

# A sheltering roof terrace

The design of roof terraces must address the problem of shelter. This includes shelter from the elements, such as the wind, which is greatly increased at roof level compared to ground level, and also shelter in the form of privacy from neighbouring houses and terraces, particularly when the roof garden is in a large city setting, such as this one situated in North London.

Here, the solution to providing shelter has been to create a perimeter barrier made out of standard sections of scaffolding, which secures a series of polycarbonate panels, nearly 3m (10ft) high in places. The panels have the advantage of being lightweight, allowing light into the terrace, but as they are opaque they also screen the views beyond the terrace. Scaffolding also creates an overhead canopy, which visually encloses the garden from the sides and allows exotic climbers to be trained over the skeletal structure.

Rick Mather's planting is extensively evergreen, with strong cuboid shapes fashioned out of clipped box, accompanied by bamboos, arbutus and the Montezuma pine, *Pinus montezumae*. His approach is to use bold, sculptural foliage, including a fine specimen *Trochodendron aralioides*. Embracing the scaffolding framework are the wandering, vine-like stems of the kiwi fruit, *Actinidia chinensis*. This is all made possible because of the sheltered haven Mather has created with the translucent panels, which filter out wind while allowing daylight to flood into the garden.

As the sun streams through the perimeter polypropylene enclosure and scaffold framework, it highlights the reflections that have been created by a glass-topped table. Glass has the reflective quality of water and is therefore an ideal material in this location.

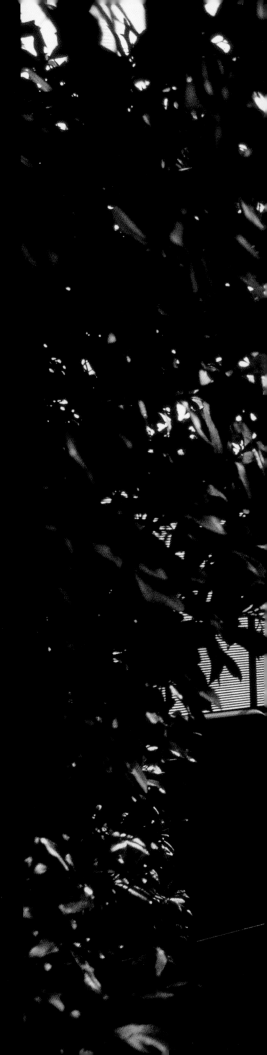

# A landscaped roof garden

A successful roof-terrace garden is one that combines views of the surrounding landscape with protection and shelter for the plants; although their growth is enhanced, they tend to suffer from the increased evaporation and from wind damage at roof level.

One solution to a roof-top planting is to create two zones: a perimeter of perforated walls or fences that is structurally strong and able to support tough climbing plants, and an inner zone that is planted with a single plant species. One excellent choice is ornamental grasses, which thrive in roof-top conditions. As well as having an ability to cope with exposure, they also exhibit a delightful quality of movement in line with the breeze. Grasses will look spectacular when in flower in late summer and they will retain their flowerheads decoratively all through the winter months.

▶ In contrast to the calamagrostis grasses planted in custom-made troughs running along the terrace's perimeter are the bottle-brush flowers of *Pennisetum alopecuroides* 'Hameln', which are set out in bulging pots.

◀ Here, an outer metal framework covered with wisteria is the backdrop for a continuous band of *Calamagrostis* x *acutiflora* 'Stricta', which culminates on a swathe of *Deschampsia caespitosa* behind specimen of river birch, *Betula nigra*.

# A roof garden of rest

Some gardens take their inspiration for design from unique situations. It may have something to do with the history of the site, or a particular interest of the owner, or perhaps a collaboration between the owner and the designer. For this roof garden there was an obvious connection between the house and the adjacent site, for the house itself sits almost within the grounds of the celebrated Victorian section of Highgate Cemetery in North London.

The owner David Pearson and the landscaper Brian Berry collaborated on this roof terrace to create a powerful expression of this unusual situation, using only a limited range of components. The focus for the design is the topiaried box plants, *Buxus*

▶ The maturing stems of *Buxus sempervirens* have been trained upright to form vertical stone-like sculptures, which make reference to the garden's unusual location.

◀ Stout white troughs which enclose the dining area are overflowing with the luxuriant foliage of *Hebe* 'Green Globe'. Its rounded form makes a pleasing contrast to the upright topiaries on the perimeter.

*sempervirens*, which have been individually sculpted to represent allegorical gravestones. Additionally, they have used other topiary that is reminiscent of the cypresses often found in European cemeteries. Within the main roof terrace a primitive stone sculpture is employed as an abstraction of simple weathered and ancient monuments, and this adds a venerable quality to the scene.

The peaceful atmosphere is further enhanced by the uplighting, which gives the composition a spiritual feeling in keeping with its situation. The weight associated with plants and soil is spread around the perimeter of the garden, as required by the structural limitations of a roof terrace.

The roof terrace exhibits at night
a dramatic gallery of three different
sculptural elements: the rounded forms
of hebe contrasting with vertically trained
box trees, all drawn together by a rough-
cut statue in a primitive style.

# A roof terrace for the workers

The ability to think laterally is a fundamental requirement in order to solve the problems inherent in a site. When the designer Topher Delaney was asked to create a space on a roof terrace in San Francisco for Bank of America employees, she invented a new and exciting garden in which plants and associated familiar objects are used in inventive ways.

Part of Delaney's inspiration was the terrace's sheer size, which meant that the design had to be bold. She therefore avoided small plants, using instead large climber-covered spheres and huge palms, interlaced with brightly coloured benches. Yet even these conspicuous features are upstaged by the "forest" of multi-coloured wind socks erected on part of the terrace. Although inanimate, they nevertheless generate movement and life, suggesting a new form of grove suited to the Californian climate. Instead of being daunted by wind and exposure, Delaney has captured and exploited their energy with a degree of wit.

This is a wonderful example of how gardens provide more conventional clients such as large corporations with a freedom of expression to external areas – a freedom unusual in the everyday office environment. It also underlines the vital role that gardens have of refreshing and recharging the minds of those who use it.

◄ On this windy terrace, the bulbous planters emerging from the raised deck give a secure base to the exotic palm trees, and also act as sculptures.

▲ The sinuous band of a bright yellow bench embraces one of the giant metal-framed and ivy-clad globes, which appear to roll across the grid of the paving.

▶▶ A series of colourful windsocks express the exposed conditions of the roof terrace, and stand like a small forest among the natural shapes of the rough boulders.

# A roof garden for executives

The roof garden of the central London headquarters of a fashion retailer was an awkward wedge-shape, overlooked by the executive suite, and with a height restriction – nothing was to rise above existing parapet level. My solution was to establish a series of spaces adjacent to the offices by constructing an inner, irregularly stepped wall, which formed a low screen in front of the parapet. Each "step" of the wall was designed to relate to the office it faced, and add another level to an otherwise flat area, providing further visual interest and creating a space for raised containers for planting. The original concrete garden floor was replaced with Western red cedar to complement the offices' interior flooring and to create a feeling of openness. The cedar was also used to construct raised planters and benches placed along the stepped wall, offering the illusion that the decking continued upwards. As these faced toward the offices, the design focus became the roof garden's centre, not the cityscape beyond. At the narrow end, in the dining area, a row of earthenware pots were positioned around the corner, repeating and emphasizing the circular patterns of the semi-circular banquette seating and round table. The repetition of the garden's elements – materials, plants and design features – produce an air of calmness throughout the space.

Silver and grey foliage plants complement the terracotta walls of polished Italian plaster. They include the New Zealand shrub, *Astelia chathamica*, with its arching strap-like leaves; tall tufted grasses such as *Stipa arundinacea*; the half-hardy honey bush, *Melianthus major*; *Agapanthus* Headbourne Hybrids; and topiary spheres of santolina, rosemary, and lavender. Silver-leaved shrubs and trees in containers and planters around the perimeter include *Elaeagnus* × *ebbingei*, and three specimen trees of *Quercus ilex*.

This is an example of a low-maintenance approach, although the plants must occasionally be pruned and fed. Spheres of box planted at the back of the benches are mulched with Scottish beach cobbles, and there is an irrigation and drainage system to cope with the high rate of evaporation and high temperatures that are characteristic of roof gardens.

▶ Low, terracotta-coloured, screen walls frame a clear central terrace of Western red cedar decking. Perimeter planting opens the centre, drawing in light and energy.

◀ A pair of box, *Buxus sempervirens*, is grown in a raised cedar-clad planter that also provides seating.

◄ In this dry and exposed location, the plants suit the conditions and also convey lightness and vitality. They include lavender, rosemary and santolina, punctuated by strappy leaves of *Astelia chathamica* and the emerging foliage of *Melianthus major*.

*Garden plan*

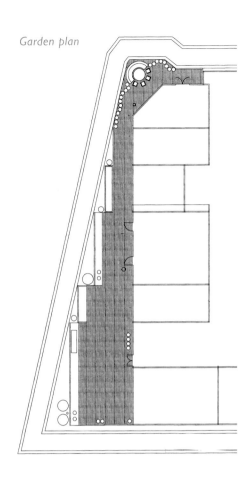

▼ The difficult geometry of this wedge-shaped roof space is resolved by the circular banquette seating, flanked on either side by sinuous chains of potted box balls, which are planted into hand-crafted terracotta.

# pools and water gardens

A simple pool cools a walled garden
of a house in Coyoacán, Mexico. The
rectangular pool was inspired by a long
water trough on the hacienda where
the architect Manuel Mestre spent his
childhood. The generous copings have
been designed at seat height, which
enhances the concept of the pool as a
focal point within the garden. The cobalt
blue-rendered wall provides a perfect
calm backdrop on which is set the
stone carved by artist Curro Ulzurrum.
Punctuated by the flowing water,
the stone creates a contemporary
fountainhead from a traditional material.

# Inspirations for pools and water gardens

Of all the elements that make a garden, water connects most strongly with the emotions – creating music, movement, sparkle, rejuvenation, reflection, coolness, stillness, mystery, and excitement, and symbolizing even more. Water has the ability to draw the eye, and so become the focus of attention in the garden. It acts as a centre of gravity, a feeling of energy flowing through the space. No wonder it is so valued in many different cultures. A central canal was a familiar cooling feature used in many classical gardens, and it is particularly effective when it is introduced into a sloping or terraced site. But water has to be treated skillfully and with restraint to achieve its magical and powerful qualities.

The level of the water is crucial: the golden rule in designing a pool is to guarantee that it is full to the brim. The effect can look very simple, but it requires intricate detailing to achieve this result. To ensure that the water is flush with the top of the adjacent paving of stone, brick, or other material, it is best to use a rigid lining such as steel, instead of a waterproof liner. This liner will achieve an abundant, understated, and uplifting image, perfect for a minimalist design. Another improvement is to design the pool so that it is

▲ Inspiration from the past: scrolled edges to this water rill at Villa Lante, Bagnaia, Italy, underline the turbulent nature of the water as it plunges down the stepped cascade. The troughs contain a shell at each step which activates the water's flow.

◄ The mysterious and special properties of water captivate everyone, including David Hockney, whose painting 'A Bigger Splash' is one of a series inspired by Californian pools.

► The water of this pool in Sydney, Australia, brims over the edge to form a virtually seamless connection with the harbour scene beyond. It creates an intriguing abstract picture that seamlessly connects the sky and the sea.

continually overflowing into a channel at one side, set a fraction below the level of the main pool and connected to a return pump. The water is kept brimming, and the constant flow also helps to clear any fallen leaves.

Water's other wonderful ability is to reflect the scene around it. Therefore a still pool that is carefully positioned can offer double value. This invariably works best when the pool is of a simple shape, well proportioned, and with the minimum of detail which would complicate the view. Sunlit reflections are the most effective. This works with any pool size, with the items to be reflected being either a well-chosen pot filled to the rim or a giant square set into surrounding grass. Reflections are strongest when the inside of the pool is very dark – painted black, perhaps, or very dark green.

Water can also separate two parts of the garden, providing a physical barrier such as a wall or hedge, but without the visual separation. A moat can create a special island within the garden. The Belgian designer Jacques Wirtz has used this idea very successfully in a garden at Kontich, Begium. The only way over the canal is via a handsome bridge, its appearance narrowed by the surrounding reeds, which heighten the experience of the separation.

But the most excitement comes from the movement of water. The sound and the sparkle are invaluable qualities, animating a restful space without affecting the mood of tranquillity. This is best seen in the classical Italian water gardens at Villa d'Este, where the terrace of one hundred fountains features carved stone gargoyles of every description. Fountain jets within the pool can create a wonderful effect, with individual jets designed to cross one another in a misty veil. In a contemporary design the jets can be set within paving, and computer operated to emerge in a series, with the water returning via drainage channels.

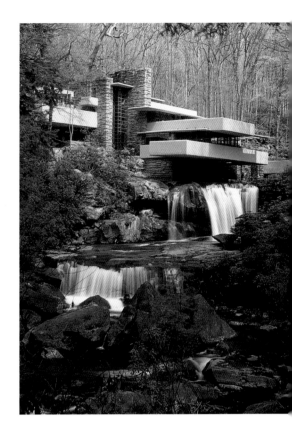

▲ Modern architecture meets nature at the Kaufmann House (Fallingwater), Pennsylvania. Frank Lloyd Wright's seminal design used reinforced concrete to create a series of terraces over a stream at the point where it breaks into a waterfall.

# A water garden as sculpture

Water makes an extraordinary contribution to a garden, and has always been highly symbolic throughout garden history. It represents abundance, and at the same time it invigorates the garden. Yet to be successful when contained in a pool, the water must be full to the brim. Anything less can have the opposite effect – lifelessness and stagnation.

Water's other great quality is its reflective power: the pool can double an image and sometimes introduce more light into enclosed areas. To achieve these requires precision and engineering. If a pool is to be completely full and not subject to evaporation, it must be designed to be continually overflowing into a subsidiary pool for recirculation. This way surface tension is created as the water hugs the pool's perimeter. The movement of water can be reduced to a minimum, without impairing its reflective quality. This has been achieved in Tadao Ando's 1997 project for Japan's Naoshima Contemporary Art Museum annex.

The annex is situated on a hilltop behind the museum and hotel complex. It is a single-storey building 40m (131ft) above the lower building. The centre is designed as an elliptical water garden, which appears as a three-dimensional water sculpture surrounded by a colonnade, and can be used as a semi-outdoor gallery. Seen from above, the pool appears to drain straight into the ocean beyond. The area is encompassed by a national park of spectacular beauty. Half of the building's volume is underground, so as not to intrude on the unspoiled surroundings. It is at one with the natural surroundings and provides a reinterpretation of nature itself in a new setting.

▶ The superb engineering of this elliptical pool creates the even tension of the water surface, which provides perfect reflections of the surrounding covered walkway and the dramatic opening to the sky.

◀ Seen from above through the elliptical opening in the landscape, the water of the pool below appears to be linked to that of the ocean beyond.

▶ In an area of outstanding natural beauty the landscape has been preserved by cutting the strong forms of the art museum and its annexe into the contours of the hillside.

Site plan

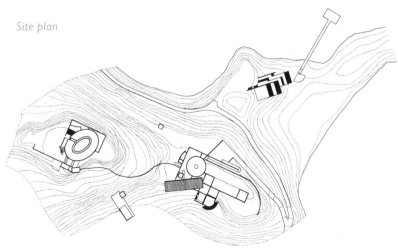

# An artful water garden

Water brings magical qualities to garden design. Some designs will integrate water into a natural scheme so that it appears as a natural feature. In the 18th century the British garden designer Capability Brown masterfully handled water within his landscape compositions so that vast artificial lakes could appear perfectly natural. As well as a complete knowledge of the engineering required, he had the most important skill – the eye for the natural composition.

By contrast the gardens of the Italian Renaissance were clearly artificial compositions. In these great gardens water was made to flow from all sides in a spectacular musical sideshow. There was no attempt at pretence. The sheer quality of the design, proportions, craftsmanship, and materials ensured fine gardens. These gardens were designed, above all, so that their owners could show off and demonstrate their wealth and power to their friends, admirers and rivals.

The 20th century has introduced its own set of problems for garden makers. We have a great knowledge of what has gone before and we know that anything can be achieved. There is the technology available to introduce water to any part of a site which the budget will allow. We know that great gardens of the past included natural-looking water features which were in fact a deceit, and we also know that obviously contrived water gardens were hugely popular. The rule is anything is possible – it is only restraint that holds us back.

Water is completely unforgiving if the levels of the site are not well handled. As well as finding its own level and therefore demonstrating clearly any details that are not absolutely flat, it will also show up any conflict with the surrounding landscape.

At night pools can be given the chance to reinvent themselves and to come alive under artificial lighting. There is a great temptation to "overcook" a lighting scheme for a pool. Water can be so reflective and seductive that it will suggest limitless opportunities for theatrical highlighting. Lighting can work well at the surrounds, in the water itself and by picking out a distant feature which will be reflected by the water. This is where a minimalist approach can point the way to a restrained but nevertheless powerful statement. As part of a project for a new house in the Napa Valley, California, the architects Powell-Tuck, Connor, Orefelt have designed a pool and adjoining guest house tower that interelates in a stunning composition. The pool and surroundings have been created from in situ concrete, and are lit at night by a network of lights, including submerged fittings. The power of the design is increased by the simplicity of the forms and the limited range of materials, all executed to a high standard.

Used as a foil, this dramatic tower arranged on the central axis is a theatrical solution for the void created by the linear pool. At night, when it is lit from below and the pool is also lit, the myriad reflections create an ethereal atmosphere.

# A scenic pool

Here is an example of the importance of keeping designs simple when they are related to a broader dramatic landscape. When asked to create a pool facing onto Lake Lucerne in Switzerland, the designer Anthony Paul wanted to keep all the elements simple in order not to detract from the magnificent scenery. The key to the design is the way that the leading edge of the pool nearest the lake has been made "frameless". As the water flows over the concealed edge it creates water tension, thereby providing the perfect mirror to the spectacular scenery. The designer has also selected only natural materials to surround the pool, and has used a limited palette of materials.

▼ The grey patina of the weathered poolside deck points toward, and echoes, the curved outline of the distant mountains beyond Lake Lucerne.

The planting has been chosen to produce a generally wild, natural mood, particularly by the use of ornamental grasses, which capture the wind beyond the rim of the pool. The one exotic element is the palm, *Trachycarpus fortunei*, in the sculptural pond that links the house to the landscape.

When introducing a swimming pool into a wider landscape, it is very important to avoid it becoming an intrusion into the untamed space. Part of the difficulty with swimming pools is their colour. Whereas the interior of ornamental pools can be treated with a dark colour, owners generally prefer swimming pools to be in a light shade of blue, to welcome the swimmer. Unfortunately, this tends to give the appearance of artificiality.

▼ As the water flows over the far edge of the pool, it creates a seamless junction with the adjacent natural planting and the Swiss mountain landscape beyond.

# Designing on special sites

New designers may start to work on undistinguished sites. It is their designs that will instill the quality and ideas. Against a neutral background there is a need to be dramatic, to lift the spirits, and to make a name for themselves before the opportunity is gone. But as their reputation grows they may be asked to work in more exceptional locations, including areas of outstanding natural beauty.

Experience also teaches restraint. It encourages confidence and with it the time to look at the site and to allow it to speak its mind. With a beautiful landscape the designer's role is not necessarily to introduce vast changes, but rather to work with the site and gently articulate its qualities. Rigorous proportions, fine materials and meticulous but restrained construction details are required. The new work has to be sympathetic to the existing surroundings, and to mirror its beauty.

When approached by the owners of this 14-acre site on the western shore of Chesapeake Bay, Maryland, to design a garden of year-round interest for their weekend home, the designers, Oehme and Van Sweden were immediately impressed by the unique and spectacular setting. They found an expertly renovated clapboard house overlooking the bay with a sweep of 125-year-old white oak, *Quercus alb*a, shading a broad lawn amidst a perimeter of dense woods.

Restraint and simplicity were the guiding lights to this design solution. In front of the house, and set within a generous expanse of decking, is the swimming pool. The rectilinear form of the pool and the direction of the decking slats tie in perfectly with the horizon line beyond. The subdued internal colour allows the pool to reflect the existing scenery, where the bay is framed by the majestic oaks and the sweep of lawn.

◀ Simple geometry and meticulous detailing do not challenge the beautiful surroundings. The horizontal direction of the decking, pool and lawn beyond echoes the seascape and horizon line.

▶ Where gardens have big landscape views, sweeps of perennial planting make a bolder statement than border-style planting. A river of *Sedum spectabile* adds a contrasting band of pink among the greenery.

The bay is the focus and there is no need to interrupt it. Any features that lie between the house and the bay are designed to echo the lines that exist, and to bring them into sharper dimension. But this does not preclude new planting. Viewing the same deck from the other direction, reveals the bold swathes of planting that the designers have introduced. Here was the opportunity to bring to the site plants that would capture the flavour of the house, the woodland, and the water in all its forms. Ornamental grasses are the starting point. When the weather is calm, their silvery forms make stunning reflections in the still pool. But when the wind blows the billowing clumps move like the waves of the ocean beyond. Their majestic forms and spectacular late-summer flower heads grasp the spirit of the place and provide a backbone for a recipe of perennials, including the purple-flowered Joe Pye weed (*Eupatorium purpureum*).

▼ Thick plantings of ornamental grasses capture the flavour of this watery scene, like a reed bed beside a mere. Dramatic plumes of miscanthus, pennisetum, and other grasses complement both the woodland backdrop and the generous plane of decking.

In another scheme, this time for the owners of quiet hillside property near Baltimore, Maryland, the designers have again turned to grasses to link water to the surrounding landscape. Here, massed bands of the upright feather reed grass (*Calamagrostis* x *acutiflora* 'Karl Foerster') provide the punctuation at the end of the pool, and allow the more rounded hillocks of the fountain grass (*Pennisetum alopecuroides*), combined with the low swathes of sedums to open up the views and form a link with fields beyond.

Both solutions appear obvious when built, but simple designs require the strongest will for they are only arrived at by rejecting the myriad design temptations that will be generated by a site of great beauty. The discipline of the minimalist approach encourages the restraint and boldness that capture the spirit of nature.

▼ Even though this pool and its terrace do not compete with the landscape views beyond, their colours are kept muted and discreet. The dense plantings of calamagrostis and other grasses, frame the pool area and realate it to the surrounding landscape.

# A blue Mexican pool

At the front of this house in Mexico City, designed by architect Javier Sordo Madaleno for himself and his family, is a courtyard which is breathtaking in its simplicity. Madaleno has rigorously reduced the design elements: the walls and floor are constructed of the same local stone, a mixture of random, irregular pieces combined with areas of sawn stone, allowing precise detailing at the junctions where two surfaces meet. The courtyard shows how natural materials can be combined with water features to create a contemporary space that incorporates classical design traditions within a minimalist composition.

There are two key elements. A tall wall at the house's entrance is rendered and painted a blood red, a colour reminiscent of pre-Hispanic times. A pool running the full width of the courtyard is connected by an underwater passage to the main bedroom's bathroom. Outside, its generous proportions and lack of adornment magnify its importance to the courtyard. Raised and set against one wall, the pool enters the wall through a defined niche, contributing to the dynamic quality of the asymmetrical yet balanced modern scheme.

By restricting the planting to glimpses of trees beyond the wall, and using only containers within, the atmosphere is of a sheltered retreat in which the walls protect the inhabitants from the external elements. The designer has been able to make maximum use of strong sun and shadow to strengthen the composition by the careful selection of textured stone, the pure proportions of the space, and the extravagant modelling of the components.

▶ The rough-edged local stone is worked into a close-fitting jigsaw puzzle of strong walling, with surprisingly precise clear-cut lines marking the niche above the pool.

◀ The mosaic pattern of the rough stone floor is continued on the raised platform and the wall beyond. The blue pool is just visible as a thin ribbon slicing through the grey stone composition. In a shady corner shallow pots are filled with luxuriant ferns.

▶▶ The pool which runs into the vivid blue niche makes a dramatic intervention in a perfect space. The stonework has been executed so that the random shapes of the stone fit together like a jigsaw, and yet have also been contrived to form severely straight lines at the junctions of one surface with another.

# A quintessential minimalist pool

Minimalist designers cannot rely on decoration and therefore have to achieve results by manipulating space, proportion and materials. The clarity and boldness of their solutions will determine the scheme's success. This is particularly important when the design of a house or garden is closely related to an unrefined natural landscape. There is always the temptation to conceal the new construction or blend it in to minimize its impact.

A minimalist design is suited to juxtaposing a simple landscape with clean design lines, and capturing the essence of the idea. This is exemplified in the new house and pool designed for a family in Majorca by the arch-exponents of minimalist architecture, John Pawson and Claudio Silvestrin. The solution for the pool, which is situated on a rooftop running away from the main house, is both breathtaking and complementary to the olive grove surrounding it. The void of the pool sweeps away from the opening incised into the house.

The details are sophisticated yet retain a simple integrity which complements beautifully the natural surroundings. The rich soil is expressed in the burnt terracotta plasterwork. The smooth stone surroundings to the pool are a refinement of the rough cut stone blocks, and a single olive tree is symbolically captured by the newly created terrace. The clean lines and superb proportions of the architecture are enhanced by the deep modelling of the house's façade, which is perfectly delineated by the strong Spanish sunlight.

◄ The exhilarating linear geometry of the pool spectacularly connects with a void in the house beyond. The cut-stone margin provides a refined contrast to the rough stone walling which retains the bank below the house.

► The simplicity of the pool's architecture relates sympathetically with the monoculture landscape of olive groves. The blue linear plane of water is a cooling and inviting element inserted into the dry surroundings.

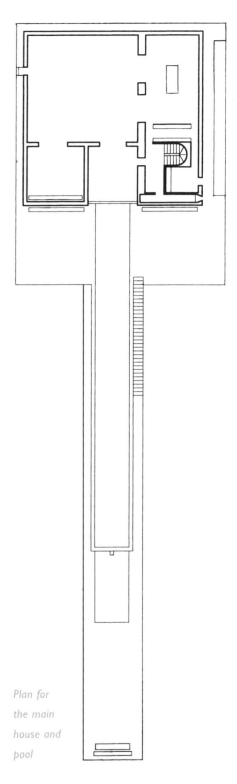

*Plan for
the main
house and
pool*

The warm colour of the crisp limestone
margins is further enlivened by rich
terracotta render on the house walls,
redolent of the Mediterranean tradition.
The deep modelling of the architecture
provides shade and dramatic shadows.

# A modernist pool

There are qualities in modernist design philosophy that perfectly suit the design of buildings situated within a natural landscape. Modern design is bold and unfussy, and these are qualities often found in nature itself. One of the particular characteristics of the natural setting for this pool, located on the north Devon coast of England, is its rugged introduction into a landscape overlooking the rough and spectacular Atlantic Ocean. A design in this situation also must be rigorous and tough, in order to reflect the atmosphere of its setting. The linear swimming pool at Baggy House is set into a sunken garden, which is approached from upper gardens leading away from the main house. Although the pool has been cut through an existing rock garden, the result manages to retain the existing character of the landscape.

One of the great features of this pool design is the relationship between vertical and horizontal planes, in particular the high pink-painted screen wall that separates the pool from the house, and ensures only glimpses of the pool before visitors descend the steps to the pool terrace. The wall has been cast in situ in concrete, a simple material that has been moulded to suit a variety of functions. While the pool sweeps away from this wall with great élan, there are features within the pool itself that add additional visual interest and entertainment value. The shallow end incorporates an underwater tunnel, which is formed by a slate bridge and a decking terrace. The screen wall also incorporates a cascade and diving board, both moulded on site from reinforced concrete.

In this impressive scheme, the architects Hudson Featherstone have used concrete throughout the scheme, varying the forms to reflect the hierarchy of the spaces to which it relates. So the concrete paving on the upper terrace is of exposed aggregate, the main terrace is ground aggregate, and the lowest level is interpreted in limestone. The inside of the pool is a white-polished cement with terrazzo, providing a clean background that allows pure reflections of the sky. The entire pool complex is a perfect combination of a serious space with entertaining qualities.

A black stone bridge just below the water's surface allows pedestrian access to the other side, or for swimmers to swim underneath it. The massive beach boulders and tamarisk hedging convey the seaside atmosphere even where the sea is not on view.

▲ In-situ concrete has been used for details at the pool's margins, in this case the seats and the table of the external dining area.

Other elements of the design have been formed in organic shapes from in situ cast concrete, which allows the scheme to fit beautifully into the adjacent hillside. The junction with the existing tamarisk hedge leading to the coast below is emphasized by a separating zone of giant river-washed boulders. There are strong echoes of the influence of the renowned architecture of the Mexican architect Luis Barragán in the simplicity and bold colour of the design, but the idea has been perfectly adapted to suit the English climate.

The scheme of the Baggy House pool is an example of how the reintroduction of modernism is all the more successful for the period of reflection that ensured, since its first wave, a result of the influence of Le Corbusier. It perfectly captures the spirit of that great architect's essential philosophy.

There has been scrupulous attention to the design of the simple materials that have been used. However, the key element that invigorates the design and lifts it from an abstract composition into something with its own life is the use of water, and the manner in which it has been employed to provide movement – first with water's reflective qualities, and then as a concealment within its depths of a whole series of unexpected design elements.

◄ The excitement of moving water is provided by a high-level, reinforced-concrete water chute, which discharges a cooling veil of water onto a timber ledge beside a concrete diving board.

▶ Individual concrete screen walls, painted in different colours, are interconnected by a simple stairway of treads cantilevered out from the main structure.

*Pool site plans*

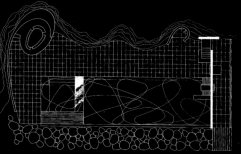

*ground plan*

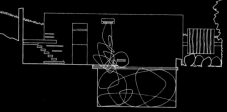

*front cross-section*

*side cross-section*

Seen from the shallow end of the pool,
the importance of the end wall is clearly
demonstrated. In addition to its sculptural
qualities, it encloses the workings of
the pool and screens the approach
from the house beyond.

# Water features and plantings

When installing a water feature in a garden, the designer can explore the contrast between liquid and solid surfaces. It is possible to consider the design of a garden as one water-filled space, out of which islands emerge – an approach that allows the creation of a minimalist design. This works most successfully when the water, hard surface and planting are at the same level, and where the design elements and number of materials are kept to a minimum. For example, it can work very well where the water is allowed to emerge through pebbles. A large area of garden can be devoted to the pebbles, with the water occurring in only part of the area contained in, and flowing from, an underground tank.

Fountains or cascades can also be introduced. This idea can be executed with other hard landscaping materials such as stone slabs, and is particularly successfully with granite setts. In such an arrangement the hard landscaping materials should be kept separate, so that water rises in the gap between the slabs where the mortar would usually be applied. Slate and granite are perfect for this treatment, because they are at their best when the wetness enhances their textures, which are not always apparent when they are dry.

With this type of design approach, the planting should be kept very simple, for example by using grasses such as *Cyperus papyrus,* which provide a vertical foil to the horizontal plane of water. Such simple schemes rely on the water's clarity; it should never be allowed to stagnate. The design should incorporate some method of recirculating the water, and it may be necessary to introduce ultraviolet filters to prevent the growth of algae.

▶ As with any simple design solution, particularly one that features water and its reflective qualities, it is vital that the surroundings are also superbly designed so that they complement the entire scene.

▲ Set within a bed of pebbles, a large boulder has been drilled to create a simple fountainhead.

◀ Painted rendered walls are a suitable background for a water garden. They will not detract from the focus of the water, and will also provide the warm tones that are so important for ensuring its attractiveness as it recirculates.

# A framed pool

This New Zealand pool scheme demonstrates that lighting, when used in conjunction with water, can remain muted but effective. At night, the rectangular openings are picked out as picture windows which frame the planting behind. These frames add a three-dimensional layering to the perimeter wall and extend the floor materials onto a vertical plane.

# country
# gardens

Country gardens can be many things:
splendid acres in undulating green
landscape, bluebell-carpeted woodland,
arid deserts or, as here, simple homes
on the seashore. The minimalist factor
of country gardens may be measured
by their treatment as pure spaces with
their own identities. The late film
director Derek Jarman lived in this
seaside fisherman's cottage, and used
locally found timbers and the deep
shingle of the beach to make a garden
perfectly in tune with its surroundings.

# Inspirations for country gardens

When designing country gardens, the challenge is always how to best to express the garden's relationship with Nature and the landscape beyond. Do the views from the garden take in a picturesque landscape such as mountains and forests, or is the scene one of the hard-working environment of a farm? Some country gardens may not have far-reaching views, and, for example, may be set within a glade or surrounded by woodland. How much intervention should then be imposed?

Country gardens of the unsettled medieval age were enclosed by high walls out of necessity to deter invaders, both human and animal, but keep in livestock and give protection to those living within. As civilization evolved and peace became more widespread, gardens were able to become more expansive, and less introverted.

When designing in the country, it is important to learn from nature, to let the site and its surroundings announce their own unique qualities. One of the great lessons of the countryside is that it is never small-minded or small scale, but its features tend to be bold – and boldly repeated – rather than introspective, with fussy detail. It is vital to understand the essence of a particular countryside. To do that it is necessary to take time out to study the region's hills and mounds, its waterways, paths, any rise and fall in the land, and the types of plants that choose naturally to grow in it. In some regions there may be great waves of wildflower planting in meadows, or forest or woodland, or there may be a more difficult terrain, such as the seaside; it is only by studying the landscape that garden-makers can see how these ideas can be borrowed and reintroduced into a garden setting.

▲ Geometry can play a significant role even in the most natural looking landscape. This line of old oak trees creates a sense of order without breaking the spell of the bucolic scene.

▶ In the garden of the Villa Lante at Bagnaia, Italy, a parterre of clipped box hedging provides an abstract representation of the countryside within the garden walls.

◀ The spiral turf maze is an ancient landscaping form connected to religious ritual, but its simple design lends itself as an abstract detail in a country garden.

▶▶ An example of how minimalism can translate to the countryside environment. This scene gives the appearance of nature, but the components have all been introduced in a regular pattern.

Local geology and materials used in vernacular architecture should also be borne in mind and used to create a garden that is in harmony with its surroundings. For example, in areas where natural stone occurs and is quarried, an ideal material is at hand to use in hard landscaping of walls and paths and making bold sculptures. In areas of clay where bricks are more commonly used, it would be appropriate to use these materials. The same applies to forested regions, where there is an abundance of timber, which can be employed in numerous ways in the garden.

Planting is crucial in the design process, and it is important to look at the plants that are native to the environment. Although garden plants should not be restricted to what is growing in the wild, they can give a lead to the style that is to be created for the garden.

Always bear in mind that country gardens must have a strong enough structure to compete with the vastness of the countryside beyond. Although many country gardens may appear natural, in the end it is their underlying framework that will enable a gardener to achieve the most successful results.

# The town and country garden

Designing a garden in the country imposes its own set of rules. Traditionally the approach was to include a mixture of styles, such as those found in a wild hedgerow. This has in part resulted from the glamorous and perhaps sentimental view of the countryside, the celebration of the pastoral and picturesque – for example, the 18th-century idea of the *ferme ornée*, the ornamental farm. With the separation between town and country narrowed, the question to be asked is how much the country garden should reflect the surrounding beauty, and how much should it also reflect the ideas and style of town life?

The successful design exploits one idea and expresses it in an uncomplicated way; it forms a relationship between buildings, garden spaces and countryside. Such an approach allows architecture and landscape to meet, thereby creating a garden space reflecting the lifestyle of the owner and yet sitting well with the landscape beyond. One solution is to enclose spaces within the garden so that they do not conflict with the natural world outside.

▶ Taking its inspiration from the horizontal emphasis of the outbuildings, bold bands of clipped box (*Buxus sempervirens*) run across the garden, punctuated by domes of santolina.

▼ The minimalist element of this room within a country garden is the superbly understated "pool". In reality it is a narrow moat surrounding a central terrace, but the use of cobbles gives the impression of rippling water.

# A Provençal country garden

A garden with spectacular views over the surrounding countryside presents designers with a problem. It would be inappropriate to enclose the garden and shut out the views beyond, and thus a design needs to be created so that the country as well as the garden near the house can be enjoyed. But what sort of design, and what plants should be included? Should it replicate what is going on in nature, or deliberately contrast with it? When the world beyond is spectacular, as in this garden in Provence, there is a danger that the garden will suffer in comparison. And how should the two areas be linked?

One solution would be to follow the lead set by Nicole de Vézian who, inspired by the plants growing wild beyond her garden boundaries, allowed them to influence the design of her terrace, as well as the garden areas near her house. Vézian reserved a place on her terrace for plants such as lavenders and santolinas that grew naturally in the wilder parts of the garden. When she grew them on the terrace, however, she clipped them in order to establish their relationship to the house. In this way Vézian was able to show her intervention in the landscape without having to introduce new plant species. The result encourages a fresh view both of wild plants and cultivated varieties near the house.

▼ The interplay of textures between balls of lavender and long-stalked lavender shrubs creates a superb garden atmosphere.

▶ This subtle mix of the evergreen foliage of lavenders and native cypress trees brings home the ambience of the countryside.

The garden at Château de Gourdon in southern France is a symphony of greens. Perched in a precipitous position above a river gorge, the garden dates chiefly from the 17th century, and enjoys majestic views of the Provençal landscape. As part of a 20th-century addition, a hedge of box, with its pleasingly rounded profile, weaves its way around clipped lime trees, and sets them apart as individual sculptures.

# The ultimate cactus garden

Cacti's sculptural forms make them ideal subjects for minimalist gardens in arid parts of the world. The Jardin de Cactus, on the Canary Island of Lanzarote, was designed by the artist and landscape architect César Manrique shortly before his death in 1992. It comprises a monoculture of 10,000 cacti and related succulents, representing more than 1,400 different species, displayed in a redundant quarry where volcanic lava ash had been extracted for local agricultural use. The quarry provided a huge semicircular arena, onto which stepped terraces were built around the edge, as in a Roman amphitheatre. Water is confined to a few small pools. In keeping with its surroundings, the island's basalt lavas are the only materials used: rusty-brown rocks form the terrace's dry-stone walls; clean-cut dark grey lava finishes the wall edges and garden steps, and is used for sinuous crazy-paved paths. Uncut lava chunks are displayed as natural sculptures in the garden's centre, echoing the tall and branching species of cacti.

► Manrique carried the cactus theme into every detail of the garden, including door handles, light fittings and this heavy iron gateway. Such well-designed details enhance the garden's important international collection of plants.

▼ Small grains of porous black volcanic ash, called *lapilli*, form a thick mulch over the planted beds. The ash draws air moisture down into the soil at night, but provides a daytime shield against water evaporation caused by the sun.

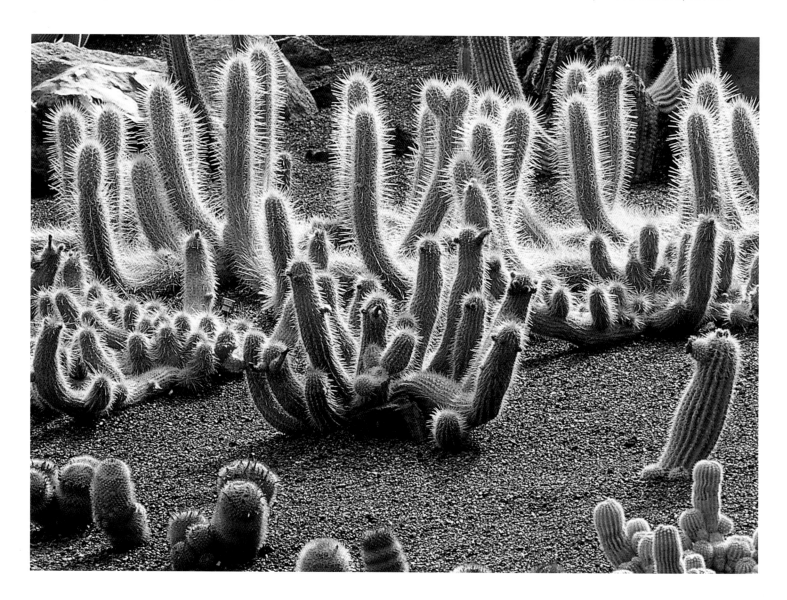

The golden barrel cactus or mother-in-law's cushion, *Echinocactus grusonii*, is very effective when planted in a bold group, with spacing between each specimen. Here, is it contrasted with the vertical shapes and silvery hairs of *Cephalocereus* cacti and chunky lava boulders.

# An American country garden

The success of designing in the countryside depends on finding a solution which works with the natural landscape, but which also introduces the colour and variety to be found in garden plants. The vastness of the American landscape, and the energy of their culture and way of life, is ideal for promoting the boldness and almost overpowering vitality that is required for American country garden design.

The designers Oehme and Van Sweden, in Washington, D.C., have made a great impact on the way gardens sit in the countryside. They have established a unique and memorable formula which involves a strong underlying plan, overplanted in the most striking style.

They first make a careful study of the landscape, the way the land lies and the natural flows, which will inspire the structure of the garden. This enables them to work with the contours and helps them accentuate the curves and rhythms of the natural features.

If the site's organization is new it can be made to appear as though it had simply grown out of the ground. Hard landscape materials are kept simple; stone or wood are laid without complication but with repetition and in rhythms that borrow from the adjoining fields. Paths are used with panache to embrace the folds of the land and to enclose or separate different areas of planting and water. This creates the perfect blank canvas for great swathes of perennial planting and ornamental grasses. The continuous sweep of one species spreading over a vast area is breathtaking and, by using as their inspiration plants which originate from the American prairies, they are able to find those which can cope visually and physically with the countryside beyond. For planting that introduces a huge number of plants and strong colour and variation between the seasons, the maintenance is reduced to manageable proportions. Much of the plantings, including huge drifts of rudbeckias, echinaceas, monardas, and grasses such as panicum and miscanthus, are late performers in the garden season. But there is a huge bonus from this selection. By keeping their structure and attractive seed heads they ensure that the gardens look good from the summer through the winter months. The plants can be cut back hard in spring to allow the new shoots to emerge and the cycle to start over again.

The results resemble huge 20th-century paintings set within a gigantic gallery. Within the compositions there are complexities and subtleties, but it is the assured and generous drifts of plants that set this scheme apart. This is a complete contrast to styles prevalent in Europe, where even the new trends in perennial planting involve a much greater variety of plants, and a look which is more akin to an intimate, self-seeded, meadow-inspired composition.

◄ A serpentine flagstone path draws the eye to great waves of planting. Perennials include pennisetum, calamagrostis, and tall miscanthus grasses, leavened with mauve clouds of eupatorium. At low level is a mass planting of autumn-flowering *Liriope muscari*.

▼ A swathe of black-eyed Susan, *Rudbeckia fulgida* var. *sullivantii* 'Goldsturm', cuts through bushy clumps of *Miscanthus sinensis* and other grasses.

◀ A vivid orange band of rudbeckia combines with purple cone flower, *Echinacea purpurea*, and a wispy veil of pale mauve *Perovskia atriplicifolia*, a strong counterpoint to the vast greenness beyond.

▲ The large quantities of single species that are used in this scheme give it the flavour of fields of flowers, rather than borders. The soft squirrel tails of pennisetum grasses contrast with the crimson mallow's bold flowers and the more wispy perovskia, while other grasses billow like clouds.

▼ Alongside the curving boardwalk that encircles the pond are bold plantings of miscanthus grasses, which, with their striking flower heads and relaxed character, make a direct connection with the wild-grown grasses growing in the fields beyond the garden .

# landscape gardens

Designing in the landscape is about
taking inspiration from the existing
planting. Here, materials of the same
colour provide a dramatic contrast of
shapes and textures. The horizontal
slats of a curved decking path respond
to the vertical spikes of rushes growing
in a watery setting.

# An urban hillock

In generating the design for a 15,240m (50,000sq ft) plaza in Minneapolis's civic centre, facing the city hall and courthouse, the landscape architect Martha Schwartz gave expression to a local culture that has been influenced by Minnesota's natural landscape.

The scheme is an example of how organic forms and natural ecology can inspire a minimalist urban landscape. The plaza is largely paved with bands of different-coloured stone that create a linear emphasis. From these a series of grass-covered, tear-shaped mounds, or hillocks, emerge, which are intended to evoke a memory of geological and cultural forms; they are a stylized expression of a field of Minnesotan glacial drumlins.

The hillocks pass through varying stages as the seasons change. In spring, some are blanketed with white narcissi, others with stripes of blue scilla. In winter, heavy snows neutralize their colour so that only their shape is revealed – a connection to their glacial origins.

*Plaza plan*

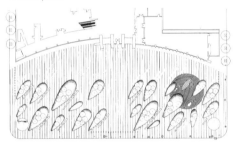

▶ Grass-covered tear-shaped mounds introduce memories of the local landscape into this hard urban scene.

▼ Seen from above, the grassy mounds cut across the strong parallel bands of striped paving. The effect is startlingly abstract.

# Architectural and natural features

In traditional 18th-century gardens, makers introduced pieces of architecture such as temples, follies and gazebos, or elaborately carved stone sculptures. The idea behind this was that the owners could demonstrate that they had captured what was otherwise an untamed landscape. The insertion of manufactured features meant, too, that they could express their impact on, and their ownership of, the wide expanse of nature. Such forms also encouraged those who were present to look at the landscape in a different way.

At that time these features had great symbolic impact, and everyone who saw them understood their meaning, as they were inspired by classical mythology. Today, in an entirely different culture, they no longer have the same relevance, yet the underlying approach can still be explored in a minimalist design. The interest in ecology and nature conservation can inspire modern designers keen to enhance or reinterpret natural features. Their interventions are more subtle than those of 18th-century garden makers, and are often stimulated by nature itself. So, for example, stones or boulders created by nature can be inspirations for garden sculpture today. Their position may sometimes be deliberately ambiguous, so that it is not always clear where nature stops and humans intervene. Yet the visitor should be encouraged to think and to re-examine the derivation of natural forms.

▼ Nature or art? This fibreglass sculpture by Gun Linblad not only echoes the colour and forms of the stone outcrop on which it sits, but also stimulates fresh thoughts on art and landscape.

◀ This garden is an entity of lines with pebbles fixed to supple stalks. An individual character to each pebble is emphasized by their separation. Wind makes them knock softly against each other.

▼ In an apparently natural landscape moss-covered boulders suddenly emit a misty vapour. Clearly a designer's intervention, but all this suggests a more primeval atmosphere.

# A French landscaped park

It is natural to want to make gardens in the countryside, but the challenge is to make ones that are truly part of the townscape: not a piece of the country brought to town, but parks and open spaces which draw inspiration from, and are unique to, the urban setting. These must be spaces that excite visually, and fit into the grain of modern metropolitan design, but they must also refresh and draw energy into the city.

In Paris, the Parc André Citroën, which opened in 1993, has provided a wonderfully stimulating range of experiences for its visitors. The landscape designers, Alain Provost and Gilles Clément, have created on the banks of the River Seine, on the site of a former car factory, a tour de force involving water throughout, and including a vast lawn, and a series of surprising experiences in the form of "serial gardens" and other ideas. The concept is entirely contemporary, and yet it complements and enlivens this great capital city. It is conceived as a serious piece of urban design, and yet remembers also to be attractive and entertaining at all times.

▼ Inspired by the cascades of Renaissance gardens and the *chadars* of Islamic and Mughal gardens, a pair of giant water staircases converge on a seating area protected from the sounds of the city.

► Rows of black irises are given an unusual urban setting as they rise through a metal framework in one of the serial gardens.

▼ A water garden is framed by enclosures of sloping walls and hedges as it faces the vast lawn and a clump of giant bamboo.

# Festival garden ideas

There is a large creative role to be played by show gardens in pointing the way to new styles of design. Particularly successful are the garden festivals held annually at Chaumont, Loire-et-Cher, France, which encourage designs that express a new way of thinking, and generate a fund of new ideas for both visitors and garden designers alike. Gardens are treated as art forms, which is exactly how the great gardens of the Italian Renaissance and later the 18th-century landscape parks were revered.

Gardens are particularly successful where there is an underlying theme or concept that can be applied to all of the garden's components. Such a theme will enable designers to think afresh about the artistic expression of individual gardens and the manner in which they can be planned in order to thrill and excite. Festival gardens may be temporary, but the ideas that they inspire influence new trends in design, and demonstrate how a simple minimalist idea, well executed, can be more powerful than a collection of different ideas.

▶ Fabric water traps suspended from a wire framework act as funnels to collect moisture and direct it into water containers at their base. They take on the form of airy, filigree sculptures in a garden set with a bisecting decking path and surrounding planting.

▼ This simple composition of stone slabs laid on edge takes the eye to the surrounding landscape. Laid in serried rows, a mist appears and disappears from the stones' bases. The moisture and angle of sunlight continuously changes their colour and texture.

▲ Rows of blue reflective globes give a hint of flowers in bloom in an otherwise un-gardened landscape. The bold stripes of paler randomly-cut stone paths cut across an irregular network of dark plum and grey gravel.

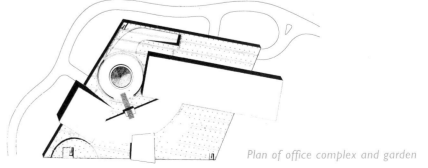

*Plan of office complex and garden*

# A Scientific Landscape

Martha Schwartz's landscape garden was designed for the Center of Innovative Technology in Fairfax, Virginia. The garden is surrounded by irregularly shaped office buildings, and the concept was to bring order to these irregular spaces. The scheme is a terrace that relates to two of the smaller office buildings and includes a copse, or bosque, of the small-leaved lime tree, *Tilia cordata*. The bosque curves gently on one side and is planted into plum-coloured crushed gravel interlaced with stripes of randomly patterned stone paths. This is overlaid by a grid of blue reflective globes, which partly reflect the glass of the surrounding architecture but also are an allusion to flowers blooming under the trees.

The success of the design lies in the fact that the ideas are kept very simple, thereby increasing the power of the scheme, and each of the elements has a fine quality in itself. The range of components – globes, paths, proportions, spaces, and the unity of the small copse – is limited, but their great advantage is their economy. Although designed for the large scale of an office complex, the use of natural materials, particularly the randomly cut paving, enables the scheme to retain the human scale so important for a garden setting.

▶ A grove of *Tilia cordata* lime trees rises directly out of the curved areas of plum-coloured gravel. The reflective, gentian-blue spheres offer a startling counterpoint to the natural greys and browns of the stone materials.

# Timber in
# the landscape

▼ Landscape architect Morgan Wheelock used black-painted fences "like brushstrokes on the landscape" to bring definition and enclosure to this horse farm in Kentucky. The trees include huckleberries and sweet gums.

◀ A timber walkway crosses a pool set within a sculpture garden. It is the offset line it describes, as it bisects the pool, that lifts the structure from a utilitarian object to a piece of sculpture itself.

► Zig-zagging through a plantation at St Francisville, Louisiana, the simplicity and flowing line of this fence sets the trees within a new pattern; in this context the device becomes an artist's intervention.

# A cosmic and earth-bound landscape

The great landscape gardens of the 18th century were largely inspired by an artistic view of nature. Classical mythology and Renaissance paintings pointed the way to the idea of the sublime landscape. The gardens of Stourhead, for example, were laid out by their owner, William Hoare, as an elegiac trail. The gardens of Stowe included a series of pavilions and sculptures which told a story, in fact a political message, which was set out for its visitors to interpret. As this was part of their culture they would have understood the nuances underlying the positioning of monuments in different parts of the landscape.

Today we cannot call on such a deep knowledge of the classics, and so if classical sculpture is used in gardens it is seen merely as decoration and judged purely on the aesthetic contribution it may add to the composition. Today gardens with an underlying story or philosophy are thin on the ground. However, when designing a large garden, of a landscape scale, it adds an extra dimension when there is a philosophy underpinning the design ideas. The larger the garden, and the more important the site, the bigger the idea needs to be. It is rare to find garden-makers with the vision to impose a strong philosophy in order to make a new garden.

But at his home on the Scottish borders the American architect, Charles Jencks, and his wife, the late Maggie Keswick, a specialist on Chinese gardens, created a new garden which has all the depth of thought and panache of the great gardens of the past.

The inspiration for this remarkable garden, now being developed further by Mr Jencks, is drawn from two sources. Mr Jencks is the author of *The Architecture of the Jumping Universe*, which expounds a new theory on cosmology. Maggie Keswick's ideas were influenced by Taoist theories of geomancy, the invisible energies in the shape of the land, and she wanted to express the bones of the earth, in this case the downland shaped by glaciers. In purely landscaping terms their garden is an awesome project of earth sculpting, which involved a reworking of substantial tracts of land, bringing in pools and bridges, fashioning earthworks into a structured pattern, and using large, specially commissioned sculptures to express their underlying themes. Although on one level it can be read as a minimalist composition, it is also an extraordinary man-made landscape of deep underlying complexity.

The view from the top of the snail mound epitomizes the magic of this extraordinary garden. Inspired by Taoist theories, the ground has been sculpted in the style of the waves and twists of natural plant forms.

▼ The junction of the snail mound and the pond demonstrates the interplay of the forms which describe the garden. Earth-moving equipment was used to excavate a series of ponds in a marshy area of the estate, allowing the excavated material to be recycled to create the spiral mound and double-wave earthworks. It is clearly an artificial landscape, and relies on a superb standard of construction and maintenance to achieve the dramatic effects of light and shadows.

◄ From the Chinese bridge, the pond and earthwork system can be seen to flow into the landscape. A garden of great depth and underlying meaning, its forms, picked out by the sun and shadows, can also be read as a great minimalist landscape.

▶ One of the spiral paths emerges from the snail mound to embrace the pond. It is a dramatic gesture, emphasized by the fragile simplicity of the grass as it curls round to a point, seeming almost to be floating on water.

# A New England river garden

Mnemonic River is a landscaped garden situated on a 10-acre site on the southern coast of Massachusetts. The designer, Janis Hall, has a background in sculpture, but now works with the wider landscape. Her sculptural approach to design is outstanding. In this garden her intention was to link the house to the sea. Earth-moving equipment was employed to create a series of waves and undulations that would mimic the ocean beyond.

The area is surrounded by forests. Much of its atmosphere comes from the way in which the shadows from the trees fall across the undulating surface. The idea was to sculpt the ground in the form of a gentle dry river bed, and to engage the background of Great Hill in the distance. The whole is a superb contemporary approach to the design of wider landscapes, and a re-interpretation of the great 18th-century landscape gardeners, whose inspiration came from both natural and artificial forms. The maritime setting also makes a connection to the natural undulations of the great Scottish links golf courses, the subtle folds and undulations of which come alive when lit by the low sunlight grazing across them. However, here at Mnemonic River, Janis Hall's approach has been to create a scene that is not only beautiful in its own right, but also encourages the viewer to look at the surroundings in a new and fresh way, and consider what is natural and what is artificial.

Hall's success lies in the way she has managed to create a landscape that appears to have had minimal intervention. She has also created a highly evocative solution to gardening on a large scale, one that seems entirely right for the present time.

The landscape was sculpted into interlocking waves and folds, which pick up the surrounding shadows and reflect an image of the sea beyond.

*Garden plan*

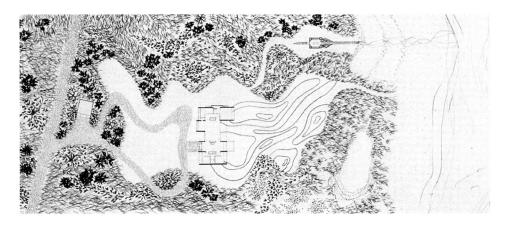

# plants and materials

Minimalism in monochrome: some
grasses lend themselves to abstract
treatment, as these mounds of blue-grey
fescue grasses admirably demonstrate.
Maintaining their compact pincushion
shape in orderly rows, they make a
splendid contrast to the organic form
and texture of the random stone path
and three massive rocks.

# Planting inspirations

There is no reason why planting within the minimalist garden needs to come from a restricted palette. In fact, the bones of the minimalist garden, conceived as an empty gallery, can be the perfect setting for showing off plants.

There are three distinctive approaches. One is to pick a plant, or a limited range of plants, that are outstanding for their sculptural form. This might be a solitary tree, planted to stand alone in a courtyard where it can be viewed as a piece of sculpture.

Another approach is to create a pattern within the garden by using groups of plants that can be trained into geometric shapes. Box and yew hedges are perfect for this style of planting, with their complex geometry of varying heights and widths, and the subtle interplay of their contrasting greens creating an abstract composition that will look attractive throughout the year.

The third approach is perhaps the most interesting for it appears to be less controlled and more relaxed. The idea is to select plants, particularly perennials and grasses, that will grow together to create a a less formal, more naturalistic look – a kind of stylized meadow. A great deal of productive research has been made into selecting plants that are of equal competitiveness and that will co-habit in an attractive and easily maintainable way, while at the same bringing a feeling of nature into the garden. Here, the planting becomes a matrix, a network that reads as a whole composition, while containing wonderful detail within it.

▶ With summer over, the cinnamon-coloured seedheads of teazels and the airy plumes of miscanthus grasses interweave harmoniously. They will remain visually interesting throughout the winter.

▶▶ Rosemarie Weisse's skilful planting at Westpark, Munich, Germany, combines ecology and artistry in equal measure, to create a naturalistic scene that relates perfectly to modern architecture.

◀ The abstract pattern of box, santolina and lavender looks crisply modern, but this planting scheme for the historic gardens of Ham House, near London, is inspired by formal 17th-century design.

▼ Jacques Wirtz's gardens are noted for their structural planting. Here, the massed planting of miscanthus grasses and the hedged enclosures are separated by the contrasting open spaces of a trim lawn.

*Digitalis ferruginea*

*Eupatorium purpureum* 'Atropurpureum'

*Euphorbia characias* subsp. *wulfenii*

1m (3ft) long. It will thrive in any deep fertile soil and is even tolerant of heavy clay soils. 2m x 1m (6ft x 3ft). CO south-west Mediterranean and Morocco
*C. scolymus*. This has elegant pointed and deeply divided leaves, and flower heads as *C. cardunculus*. Both species make striking architectural plants that combine well with brick walls and paving. H and S 1.2m x 1m (4ft x 3ft). CO rocky slopes and dry grasslands of southwest Europe

## Digitalis spp.
*D. ferruginea*. A short-lived perennial with pale gold, brown-veined flowers which are borne in dense slender spires in mid summer above rosettes of long, dark green leaves. It makes a good punctuation mark when grown in a grass and perennial border, and combines well with grasses such as *Calamagrostis* 'Karl Foerster'. H and S 1.2–1.5m x 30cm (4–5ft x 12in). CO woodland, scrub, and rocky sites in Turkey, Balkans, and Lebanon
*D. laevigata*. Small, orange-white flowers with brown-purple veining and a white lip are produced in summer on stiff upright stems above rosettes of leathery dark green leaves. Prefers full sun and a well-drained soil. H and S 1m x 60cm (3ft x 24in). CO west and central Balkans

*D. lanata*. A short-lived perennial with off-white to pale caramel-coloured flowers marked with brown veining. H and S 75cm x 45cm (30in x 18in). CO Italy, Balkans, Hungary, and Turkey
*D. parviflora*. Produces many stout spires of densely borne, chocolate-coloured flowers above a basal rosette of large elongated leaves. H and S 75cm x 45cm (30in x 18in). CO northern Spain

## Echinacea purpurea
A variable species with large, broadly horizontal, daisy-like flowers ranging from white to rich mauve-crimson, with central cones of orange-brown. It has a long-flowering season from mid summer to autumn. Its stiff branching stems need no staking. Combines well with *Miscanthus malepartus*. Prefers a fertile soil and open sunny site. H and S 1.5m x 60cm (5ft x 24in). CO eastern Australia

## Echinops ritro
A statuesque plant with stiff, powdery-white stems carrying golf-ball size, dark steely blue spheres of flowers well clear of sheaves of jagged green leaves with silvery undersides. Grow in full sun in well-drained soil in a gravel garden or border with tall molinias and stipas. H and S 1.20m x 75cm (48in x 30in) CO garden origin

## Eryngium agavifolium
This exotic-looking evergreen foliage plant is most effective when used singly in Mediterranean-style plantings or gravel gardens. It forms large rosettes of sharp, spiny, light green leaves from which rise strong, sinuous branched stems carrying cylindrical greenish-white flower heads. H and S 1–1.5m x 75cm (3–5ft x 30in). CO Argentina

## Eupatorium purpureum 'Atropurpureum'
A statuesque and elegant, perennial with great umbels of deep rosy-purple borne on stiff dark stems in late summer. Gives considerable height and bulk to planting schemes, and makes an excellent partner for big grasses such as *Miscanthus sacchariflorus*. H and S 2.2m x 1m (7ft x 3ft) CO damp woodland of eastern North America

## Euphorbia characias subsp. wulfenii
Glaucous foliage and large cylindrical heads of greenish-yellow flowers combine to form a stately clump which makes a fine specimen plant for the gravel garden or container. A useful shrub-like plant for urban gardens which retains its form year round. Tolerates semi-shade, but not wind. H and S 1.2m x 1m (4ft x 3ft). CO western Mediterranean

*Filipendula rubra* 'Venusta'

*Gaura lindheimeri*

*Knautia macedonica*

## Ferula communis 'Gigantea'

A stately plant which from late spring to summer sends up thick, purple-tinted stalks bearing large umbels of yellow flowers from a mound of dark, finely-cut foliage. Grow in any well drained soil in full sun. Attractive brown seed heads appear in late summer and last well into autumn, providing height and structure as surrounding plants die down. H and S. 2–3m x 60cm (6–9ft x 24in). CO dry, stony sites in the Mediterranean

## Filipendula rubra 'Venusta'

Fluffy plumes of showy, pure-pink flowers are held well clear of large jagged leaves for several weeks in late summer. The strong erect stems require no staking and should be left standing through the autumn to display the green seed heads. Requires a retentative soil in full sun or part shade and will thrive alongside a waterside planting. H and S 2m x 1.2m (6ft x 4ft). CO eastern United States

## Foeniculum vulgare, Foeniculum vulgare 'Purpureum'

*F. vulgare.* This has fine, feathery, light green, aromatic foliage that creates a hazy foil for the flowers of mid-height perennials such as *Eryngium planum*. It thrives in a sunny site with a fertile, well-drained soil, but will tolerate some shade. Plant in snaking sweeps, or as

isolated specimens within the border. H and S 1.8m x 45cm (6ft x 18in). CO Mediterranean *F. v.* 'Purpureum'. Similar to *F. vulgare*, but with dark bronze, silky, hair-like foliage, and ochre-yellow flower heads. A good foil for the glowing red flowers of *Knautia macedonica*. H and S 1.8m x 45m (6ft x 18in). CO southern Europe

## Gaura lindheimeri

A light, airy plant, producing delicate pink-flushed white flowers on glaucous grey stems among slender, willow-like leaves. When planted en masse it creates billowing clouds of dancing flowers in late summer to autumn. Thrives in full sun and a well-drained soil, and is an ideal subject for the gravel garden where it combines well with *Foeniculum vulgare* 'Purpureum'. H and S 1.5m x 90cm (5ft x 36in). CO southern United States

## Helianthus salicifolius

Valued more for its foliage than its flowers, this tall perennial has strong branching stems bearing many narrow, willow-like leaves, and golden-yellow flowers, which are produced from late summer to autumn. This is a plant of architectural stature to be grown with big grasses such as *Miscanthus sacchariflorus*. Prefers a retentive soil in sun or semi-shade. H and S 2.5–3m x 60cm (8–9ft x 24in). CO southern-central United States

## Helleborus argutifolius

Forms mounds of smooth, grey-green, spiny-edged leaves, making good ground cover in semi-shade in a humus-rich, free-draining soil. In winter it sends up clusters of nodding, apple-green, cup-shaped flowers which last well into spring. This is an elegant woodland perennial, which is also suited to growing on banks or raised beds where its drooping flowers and spreading habit are well displayed. H and S 60cm x 45cm (24in x 18in). CO maquis scrub in Corsica and Sardinia

## Iris pallida subsp. pallida

The foliage of this plant is broad-bladed and of a striking blue-green, and lasts well into the autumn. Scented pale lavender-blue flowers are borne from late spring to early summer. Plant alone en masse with a polished plaster wall to provide a backdrop and to set off its spiky form, or in a gravel planting with verbascums and salvias. H 1.2m (4 ft). CO Adriatic coast

## Knautia macedonica

Provided it has a warm, sheltered site with well-drained soil this scabious-like plant will produce its glowing, dark crimson flowers held on long, wiry stems for many months from summer into autumn. It is even happy in a chalk or limy soil.

*Lilium candidum*

*Linum narbonense*

*Opuntia robusta*

H and S 60cm x 45cm (24in x 18in).
CO scrub and open woods and the Balkans

## Liatris spicata

This colourful, robust perennial requires
little attention and flowers for many months
throughout the summer. Numerous mauve-
pink tassels make up bottle-brush flower
spikes borne on upright stems above grassy
foliage. Grow in fertile, moist but well-drained
soil in full sun with medium-height grasses
such as molinias and panicums. H and S
60–90cm x 45cm (24–36in x 18in).
CO damp meadows and North America

## Lilium spp.

*L. candidum.* This tall, graceful species bears
simple, white, fragrant flowers with orange
stamens in early to mid summer. Grow in
good, well-drained alkaline soil in a shaded
border as an accent plant, or as a striking
specimen for a container. H 1.5m (5ft).
CO south-eastern Europe and eastern
Mediterranean
*L. martagon.* This species is more suited
to naturalistic plantings, and will establish
well in grass in semi-shade. The scented
waxy flowers are purple-pink and darkly
spotted, and borne on long, slender
stems in early summer. H 1.2 m (4ft).
CO Swiss Alps

## Melianthus major

This beautiful foliage plant has glaucous,
silvery, drooping leaves with jagged edges
which provide an excellent foil for purple-
flowered plants like *Lavandula* 'Hidcote'. It
also makes a fine specimen container plant.
H and S 1m x 75cm (3ft x 30in). CO South
Africa (Northern, Western, and Eastern Cape)

## Monarda 'Ruby Glow'

The flowers of this plant are of an unusual
luminous deep red with a hint of purple,
and are produced from mid to late summer.
Relatively mildew-resistant, it will perform
best in a fairly fertile soil that does not dry
out in summer in full sun or very light shade.
It combines well with tall grasses which
provide a foil for the dark seed heads and
persistent winter silhouette. H and S 1.2m x
45cm (4ft x 18in). CO United States

## Linum narbonense

The simple, clear slate-blue flowers are very
striking when these plants are grown en
masse in full sun. At a distance they give
the effect of a rippling surface of water. The
flowers are produced throughout summer
on fine stems with greyish-green leaves. It
prefers a humus-rich, well-drained peaty soil.
H and S 30–60cm x 45cm (12–24in x 18in).
CO west and central Mediterranean

## Opuntia ficus-indica, Opunta robusta

*O. ficus-indica.* This perennial cactus has the
flattened stem profile of the prickly pear, with
silvery-blue oval segments and saucer-shaped
yellow flowers in late summer, followed by
oval fruits. Grow in gardens with a desert-like
climate, or treat as a tender conservatory
plant with a minimum temperature of 10°C
(50°F). A striking but containable architectural
plant, it needs plenty of light and a free-
draining soil. H and S 1.5m x 70cm (5ft x
28in). CO desert regions of the Americas
*O. robusta.* The prickly pear is a perennial
shrubby or tree-like cactus with flat, thick,
oblong to rounded, bluish-green segments.
Masses of shallow, bowl-shaped yellow flowers
in late spring and summer are followed
by spherical to elliptical, deep-red, edible
fruits. It needs sun and a well-drained soil.
H and S 5m (15ft) or more. CO Mexico

## Pachysandra terminalis

This plant tolerates most soils, making it a
reliable provider of a shiny ground cover in
partial or full shade. It has dark green leathery
leaves with jagged edges, and whorls of small
white flowers in spring. Neat and compact, it
is suitable for oriental-style plantings and
combines well with bamboos and azaleas.
H and S 20cm x 30–45cm (8in x 12–18in).
CO East Asia and eastern United States

*Persicaria affinis* 'Superba'

*Rudbeckia fulgida* var. *sullivantii* 'Goldsturm'

*Tiarella cordifolia*

## Persicaria affinis 'Superba', Persicaria amplexicaulis 'Alba'

*P. affinis* 'Superba'. This plant spreads rapidly along the ground to form a tangled mat of foliage from which pale pink flower spikes arise from early to late summer. In autumn the light green leaves take on coppery-red tints. It grows best in shade and is very useful in woodland, or in wilder plantings. H and S 15cm x 60cm (6in x 24in). CO Himalayas

*P. amplexicaulis* 'Alba'. A beautiful, tall, white-flowering form sending up tapering spires of flowers from a dense and bushy base of leaves throughout the summer and well into the autumn. The strong stems require no staking. This species also prefers a semi-shaded site. H and S 1.2m x 90cm (4ft x 36in). CO Himalayas

## Phlomis russeliana

This large perennial has large, rough leaves, dark green above and greyish-green beneath, which provide excellent ground cover. In the summer it sends up stout flower stems clothed in whorls of buttery-yellow, hooded flowers. It will thrive in full sun in a well drained soil, and is a good subject for Mediterranean or gravel plantings. H and S 1m x 60cm (3ft x 24in). CO scrub and woodland in Turkey

## Phlox paniculata 'Blue Paradise'

This has an unusual colour which changes depending on the amount of sunlight it receives. In a shaded border or on an overcast day it takes on a purply-mauve hue, while in brighter sunshine it is more magenta-pink. The flowers are produced from late summer into autumn and combine well with other late-flowering perennials such as *Aconitum carmichaelii*, and tall grasses such as *Miscanthus sinensis* 'Gracillimus'. H and S 90cm x 45cm (36in x 18in). CO garden

## Rudbeckia fulgida var. sullivantii 'Goldsturm'

Long, pointed yellow petals fall back from a central black cone held at the end of strong stems. These flowers are borne from late summer into autumn on a plant that prefers some moisture in the soil, and an open sunny site. H and S 60cm x 12cm (24in x 5in). CO garden origin

## Salvia officinalis

A mound-forming evergreen sub-shrub with soft aromatic silver-grey leaves that send up spikes of purple flowers in summer. It will tolerate most sites but does best in free-draining soil in full sun. Ideal for growing in pots or raised beds where it will spread over edges and spill over walls. It is one of a huge

genus, with over 900 species. H and S 75cm x 75cm (30in x 30in). CO Mediterranean

## Sedum telephium 'Matrona'

A beautiful and useful plant which provides interest throughout much of the year, from the fresh lime-green, tightly furled leaves emerging in a neat dome in the spring, to the rose-pink flower heads in the summer, to the fading reddish-brown tones of autumn. The strong stems need no staking and the flat flower heads make a fine contrast with *Stipa tenuissima*. Also recommended is *Sedum spectabile*. H and S 75cm x 60cm (30in x 24in). CO garden origin

## Thalictrum rochebruneanum

A tall, stately plant for a shaded site in a rich soil that does not dry out in summer. Produces clouds of small, fluffy, purple-mauve, flowers in plumes at the top of strong, upright lightly glaucous stems with fine airy leaflets. Combines well with *Eupatorium purpureum* and *Miscanthus sacchariflorus*. H and S 2m x 60cm (6ft x 24in). CO Japan

## Tiarella cordifolia

Has light green, bronze-veined leaves that take on reddish hues in winter, and airy panicles of delicate, creamy-white flowers in the spring. It thrives in the shade and

*Veronicastrum virginicum*

*Astelia chathamica* 'Silver Spear'

*Ceanothus arboreus* 'Trewithen Blue'

tolerates most soils even those that are fairly dry. It is evergreen in milder areas. A good subject for woodland plantings, and is most effective when planted en masse and allowed to spread. H and S 25cm x 25cm (10in x 10in). CO North America

**Verbena bonariensis**

The clusters of small purple flowers held on stiff branching stems create a haze of colour when this tall verbena is planted through beds of grasses and perennials. It needs no staking. When it is grown in full sun and a free-draining soil it will flower from the summer well into the autumn months, contrasting beautifully with the fading flower heads of tall grasses. H and S 1.5m x 45cm (5ft x 18in). CO damp grassland in South America

**Veronicastrum virginicum**

This tall, elegant perennial sends up dense spires of white flowers for a long period throughout the summer. It is very effective when planted in sweeps through massed perennials and grasses, providing a strong vertical accent to contrast with the horizontal forms of flowers. Prefers a moist but well-drained soil in sun or semi-shade. H and S 1.2m x 45cm (4ft x 18in). CO woods and scrub, eastern North America

**Vitis vinifera 'Purpurea'**

This ornamental grape vine has young leaves that are pale and downy, turning mulberry red in summer and rich purple in autumn. The fruit is purple-black with a blue bloom. It makes a striking plant when grown over a pergola in a sunny spot, where the sun will catch the leaves and make them glow. H 9m (27ft). CO northern hemisphere

## Shrubs

**Astelia chathamica**

This plant makes a spiky clump of sword-shaped, arching grey-green leaves with a silvery bloom. In large spaces, it creates in impressive effect when planted en masse alone or with grasses. Thrives in full sun or semi-shade in a fertile soil. *A. c.* 'Silver Spear' is a fine variety. H and S 1.2m x 2m (4ft x 6ft). CO New Zealand, Tasmania, and islands in the South Pacific

**Ceanothus arboreus**

In early summer in a sheltered, sunny spot, this fast-growing large shrub is covered in deep, vivid-blue flowers borne abundantly in large panicles. It can be trained against a sunny wall where its flowers will be most dramatically displayed. *C. a.* 'Trewithen Blue' is a superb variety. H and S 6m x 8m (18ft x 24ft). CO California

**Elaeagnus x ebbingei**

This robust shrub has glossy, dark green leaves which are silvery and downy beneath, and gingery young shoots which bear small very fragrant flowers from mid autumn through to spring. Vigorous and fast-growing, it can be used as a specimen or to make a dense hedge or screen, and will withstand coastal conditions. H and S 3m x 3m (9ft x 9ft). CO southern Europe and Asia

**Fouquieria splendens (Ocotillo)**

This succulent has long, graceful, thorny stems covered in bright green leaves and bearing large panicles of scarlet blooms. Grow in a conservatory with a minimum temperature of 10°C (50°F) in a very free-draining soil, and keep absolutely dry during summer. H and S 10m x 2m (30ft x 6ft). CO desert regions of United States and Mexico

**Hebe salicifolia**

An open, rounded, and graceful evergreen shrub, with slender lanceolate bright green leaves and long racemes of white or lilac-tinged flowers throughout summer. Grow in any well-drained soil in a sunny spot, as a specimen or with other contrasting shrubs such as yuccas. *H.* 'Green Globe' is a good variety. H and S 2.5m x 2.5m (8ft x 8ft). CO New Zealand (South Island)

*Lavendula stoechas*

*Magnolia grandiflora* 'Exmouth'

*Santolina chamaecyparissus* (syn. *S. incana*)

## Juniperus scopulorum 'Skyrocket'

A striking conifer which has reddish-brown bark and aromatic glaucous blue foliage, but is most remarkable for its pencil-thin form. It makes an excellent specimen plant, and is also effective in solitary groups, providing a strong vertical accent to contrast with planes of closely cut grass. H and S 8m x 75cm (24ft x 30in). CO Rocky Mountains from British Columbia to Arizona and Texas

## Lantana var.

These tender shrubs are grown for their brightly coloured flower heads which are borne profusely thoughout the summer. The flowers of *L. camara* range from yellow to orange to red, while those of *L. montevidensis* have a pinker hue. Grow in containers in a conservatory and bring outside in the summer. H and S 1–2m (3–6ft). CO South America

## Lavandula

These small, silver-leaved shrubs grown for their distinctive aromatic spikes of blue-purple flowers. Some species are used to form low hedges (*L.* 'Hidcote'), others make good container plants (*L. stoechas*) – all work well in the gravel garden, thriving in full sun and a well-drained soil. H and S 45–75cm x 45–75cm (18–30in x 18–30in). CO Europe

## Magnolia grandiflora

In mild areas this evergreen will grow to a medium-size tree, but in cooler regions it is best grown against a warm and sunny wall where the large, creamy white flowers will be profusely produced. The thick, leathery, shiny leaves give the plant a lush, tropical, exotic look, with strong Mediterranean associations. It makes a good courtyard plant, as it combines well with stonework. *M. g.* 'Exmouth' is to be recommended. H and S 3m x 3m (9ft x 9ft) after 10 years; ultimately 5m (15ft) tall. CO south-eastern United States

## Punica granatum

The pomegranate is a large, handsome, semi-evergreen shrub or small, bushy tree has shining green leaves which are bronzed when young, and showy orange-red flowers which are borne in late summer. Grow it in a pot in a well-lit conservatory, and move it outside in the summer if required. The fruits are borne in autumn, but rarely ripen in cooler regions. H and S 2.5m x 2m (8ft x 6ft). CO western Asia

## Rosmarinus officinalis

This spreading, open shrub contrasts well with the neat clipped forms of both buxus and santolina. The silvery-grey leaves are aromatic, and the flowers are small and

purple-blue and borne throughout summer, after an initial flush in spring. Thrives in a hot, dry position and makes a fine subject for the gravel garden or container. H and S 1.5m x 1.5m (5ft x 5ft). CO dry coastal areas around the Mediterranean

## Salix exigua

A large, graceful willow with wand-like stems bearing shimmering, silvery-grey, silky textured leaves. Has an almost bamboo-like quality, giving movement to waterside plantings as it sways in the wind – very effective when planted alone en masse, or in drifts at the edge of woodland. Flourishes in any good loamy or damp soil, and prefers full sun. H 4m (12ft) with an indefinite spread. CO western North American and northern Mexico

## Santolina chamaecyparissus (syn. S. incana)

This plant forms a low mound of woolly, silvery, feathery foliage which can be kept neat and compact with regular clipping. The bright lemon-yellow flowers are produced from mid summer. Can be grown to form a neat low hedge, as a dome-shaped container plant, or in a gravel garden. Prefers full sun and a well-drained soil. H and S 60cm x 60cm (24in x 24in). CO Pyrenees and southern France

*Buxus sempervirens*

*Carex pendula*

*Cortaderia richardii*

## Yucca filamentosa

This is a stemless species with erect or arching sword-shaped blue-green leaves which have a slight white bloom and edges adorned with fine, white curly threads. The creamy-white flowers are borne in erect, cone-shaped panicles up to 2m (6ft) high in mid to late summer. Grown in well-drained soil in full sun this makes an excellent gravel-garden plant, or specimen for a cobbled courtyard. H and S 60cm–2m x 75cm (24in–6ft x 30in). CO southern United States and Central America

## Hedging Plants

### Buxus sempervirens spp.

A genus of about 70 species, this is a a widely grown evergreen plant with small, glossy, dark leaves which clip well to make formal hedges and geometrical shapes. Box balls planted en masse or in plain containers are very effective at creating an instant structure within a planting scheme, and also provide an interesting contrast when planted within a grass border.
*B. sempervirens.* The most common form of box used for hedging. Has luxuriant dark green glossy leaves, and the ability to grow and form a healthy looking hedge in the most unpromising situations. H and S can reach 5m x 5m (15ft x 15ft). CO southern Europe,

North Africa, West Asia, and calcareus soils in Great Britain
*B. s.* 'Handworthiensis'. Is suitable for creating tall hedges, its habit being upright at first and spreading with age. H and S 1.5m x 1.5m (5ft x 5 ft). CO Europe, North Africa, and Turkey
*B. s.* 'Suffruticosa'. A dwarf shrub which lends itself well to clipping. Ideal for creating low compact hedges. H and S 1m x 1.5m (3ft x 5ft). CO Europe, North Africa, and Turkey

### Taxus baccata

This coniferous evergreen yew has very dark green, almost black, needles, and is good for creating large, dense hedges. It has an almost architectural weight and solidity, providing invaluable structure to the layout of a garden. Grow in any reasonable soil, in sun or shade. H and S 1.5m x 60cm (5ft x 24in) after 5 years; ultimately 20m (60ft) tall. CO chalk formations in Europe, western Asia, and Algeria

### Tilia cordata

This is a medium-size tree that can be pleached to form a "hedge on stilts". This is done by training in young, flexible branches to grow either as a flat, narrow hedge, or to create a more box-like effect. The heart-shaped leaves are glossy and dark green, and the overall effect is less formal and more

open than that created by pleached hornbeam. H and S 7m x 3m (21ft x 9ft); ultimately 20m (60ft) tall. CO Europe

## Grasses and Sedges

### Carex pendula

This evergreen has broad, high-arching leaves, which are fresh green when young and aging to leathery dark green, and graceful pendulous flower heads. It grows well in shade or semi-shade with woodland plants like *Astrantia major* 'Claret', or it can be planted along the base of a clipped yew hedge where the repeated effect of the arching flower stems is highlighted. H and S 1m x 1m (3ft x 3ft). CO woodland and marshes, Europe and North America

### Cortaderia richardii

This tall, elegant, evergreen grass has fine leaves with a cream central vein, and arching light brown seed heads which stand for many weeks into the autumn. It flowers in mid to late summer, producing delicate silvery plumes on arching stems well above the clump of basal foliage. It thrives in a warm sunny spot on well-drained soil, and makes a fine accent plant among perennial and grass plantings. H and S 2.5m x 1.8m (8ft x 6ft). CO New Zealand

Festuca glauca

Miscanthus sinensis 'Gracillimus'

Panicum virgatum

## Cyperus papyrus

A dramatic, towering sedge with tall, strong, leafless stems which carry huge airy umbels of pale, oat-coloured spikelets in summer. A tender plant for very moist soil, it makes a graceful conservatory plant when there is protection from direct sun. In warmer areas grow in shallow water with rocks or a pebble mulch to hide the base of the plant, and to accentuate the oriental elegance of its form. H and S 3–5m x 1m (9ft–15ft x 3ft). CO Egypt

## Festuca glauca

A small, blue-leaved evergreen grass with a distinctive tufted form. Looks very effective when planted to form a mass of grassy hummocks, especially when used with modern landscaping materials such as beach cobbles. Plant in full sun in poor, free-draining soil to allow the best leaf colour to develop – it will not tolerate a damp soil, especially in winter. H and S 30cm x 20cm (12in x 8in). CO limestone northern and southern temperate regions

## Miscanthus sacchariflorus, Miscanthus sinensis 'Gracillimus'

*M. sacchariflorus.* A dramatic, vigorous grass that derives its name from its broad-bladed foliage which resembles sugar cane. It quickly bring great height to a border within a short

time. Thrives in full sun and a moist soil, but needs some protection from strong winds. Combines well with water and with tall perennials such as rudbeckias. H and S 2m x 1.5m (6ft x 5ft). CO South-East Asia

*M. sinensis* 'Gracillimus'. Has very narrow, gracefully arching leaves in dense, compact clumps which are a uniform grey-green with a central white line. Impressive when planted in bands en masse, or on either side of a pathway to create a tunnel effect. H and S 1.5m x 60cm (5ft x 24in). CO South-East Asia

## Molinia caerulea subsp. 'Karl Foerster', Molinia caerulea subsp. 'Edith Dudszus'

All molinias prefer a damp, rather acid soil. They can be grown either in a mixed herbaceous border or in a woodland garden.

*M. caerulea* ssp. *arundinacea* 'Karl Foerster'. An upright grass forming green clumps that send up tall, golden-brown, delicate arching flower spikes in late summer to autumn. Makes a neat, non-invasive clump. The flower heads give a light and airy effect; in the late autumn the plant turns subtle shades of golden-yellow. H and S 2.2m x 60cm (7ft x 24in). CO Europe, north and south-west Asia

*M. c.* subsp. *a.* 'Edith Dudszus'. This grass makes a compact, arching clump with upright stems carrying unusual dark flower heads. It combines well with asters and achilleas.

H and S 90cm x 30cm (36in x 12in). CO Europe and south-west Asia

Also recommended: *M. c.* subsp. a. 'Windspiel' and *M. arundinacea* 'Zuneigung'. The former has more substantial flower heads than 'Karl Foerster'; the latter, which is similar to 'Windspiel', has more delicate seed heads.

*M. c.* subsp. *a.* 'Transparent'. Has stronger flower heads and is less likely to be damaged by severe weather than other members of this subspecies. The mass of tiny, delicate flowers creates an airy haze after rainfall or a heavy dew. H and S 2m x 60cm (6ft x 24in). CO Europe

## Panicum virgatum

This has distinctive, grey-green leaves and is stiffly upright. The flower heads bear small, widely spaced spikelets that give a misty effect when seen from a distance en masse. Plant in a dry soil in full sun among other grasses and perennials for a strong vertical accent. Starts growth late in the season and retains its dead foliage into the winter. H and S 1.5m x 90cm (5ft x 36in). CO North and Central America

## Pennisetum alopecuroides

Forms domes of robust, arching, emerald-green foliage, and in late summer to autumn is covered in distinctive purple-brown, bottle-brush flower heads. Grow at the edge

*Stipa barbata* 'Silver Feather'

*Chusquea culeou*

*Acacia dealbata*

of a border or in a gravel garden. *P. a.* 'Hameln' has finer, paler foliage, is more compact, and produces its purple flowers earlier. H and S 60–90cm x 60cm (24–36in x 24in). CO eastern Australia and eastern Asia

**Stipa arundinacea, Stipa barbata 'Silver Feather', Stipa gigantea, Stipa tenuissima**
*S. arundinacea.* Makes loose clumps of shiny, orange-red leaves, whose colour intensifies during winter. In autumn it bears open airy panicles of purplish-green flower spikes on overhanging stems. Contrasts well with the clipped domes of santolina or box. H and S 1m x 1.2m (3ft x 4ft). CO New Zealand
*S. barbata* 'Silver Feather'. This is an elegant, arching, feathery grass with white flower heads on silvery stems. It prefers full sun. H and S 75cm x 75cm (30in x 30in). CO south-western Europe
*S. gigantea.* A fine front-of-the-border grass whose tall, waving flower stems give glimpses of plantings beyond. Flowers mature from an oaty-brown to pale straw-gold, and are held above evergreen clumps of leaves. H and S 2.5m x 1.2m (8ft x 4ft). CO Spain and Portugal
*S. tenuissima.* A beautiful grass with very fine, hair-like leaves with a pale straw colour. Plant en masse, where it will sway and billow in the wind. H and S 60cm x 25cm (24in x 10in). CO southern United States and Mexico

## Bamboos

**Chusquea culeou**
This slow-growing evergreen bamboo makes a broad, dense clump, occasionally up to 9m (27ft) high. The cane sheaths are a shining white in their first year, contrasting with the canes which are of a deep olive green. Thrives in a sunny position in a free-draining soil. H and S 6m x 2.5m (18ft x 8ft). CO Chile

**Fargesia murieliae (syn. Sinarundinaria murieliae)**
An elegant evergreen bamboo forming rounded, spreading clumps of outward arching canes. The young canes are a bright pea-green and combine with the long narrow leaves to give a fresh, airy effect. As they age the canes become blue-grey and banded with yellow. Plant with some shelter from strong sun and cold winds, which may damage the foliage, in a moist or damp soil. Makes an imposing specimen plant. H and S 4m x 1.5m (12ft x 5ft). CO China

**Phyllostachys aurea, Phyllostachys nigra**
*P. aurea.* This evergreen plant forms graceful clumps of canes which are bright green at first, maturing to pale creamy-yellow, bearing long, pointed, light green leaves. In full sun the canes turn a dull yellow, so for best colour it should be grown in light shade in a fairly moist soil. Makes a refined specimen when grown in a pebble mulch in a Japanese garden. H 2.5–3.5m (8–11ft) with an indefinite spread. CO China
*P. nigra.* A striking evergreen bamboo with an upright form and graceful arching habit that makes it suited to planting in containers. Spreads slowly to form a large clump, but is not as invasive as many bamboos. The canes are green the first year, becoming mottled dark purple and eventually a smooth jet black. The plant imparts elements of oriental minimalism when it is planted as a specimen, or as a dramatic black bamboo. H 3–5m (9–15ft), with an indefinite spread. CO China and Japan

## Trees

**Acacia dealbata**
This small, delicate-looking, evergreen tree has fern-like blue-green leaves, and clusters of fluffy, golden, fragrant flowers borne in mid spring. Given the right situation – a sheltered, sunny position with free-draining soil in a mild area of the country – this will quickly grow to form an upright, open, elegant specimen. H and S 15m x 30m (50ft x 100ft) after 5 years. CO south-eastern Australia and Tasmania

*Betula utilis var. jacquemontii*

*Eriobotrya japonica*

*Eucalyptus parvifolia*

### Acer mono (syn. A. pictum)

This is a rounded deciduous tree whose leaves are nearly heart shape and have tapered lobes, and turn from bright green to yellow in the autumn. The tree bears clusters of greenish-yellow flowers. H 12–15m (36–50ft). CO Japan, China, Manchuria, and Korea

### Betula utilis var. jacquemontii

This birch has beautiful white papery bark which peels to reveal a pinkish layer beneath. It is most striking in winter without its leaves, with the stark white of the branches showing up against a clear blue sky. This elegant tree looks effective when grown in groups in grass, or in woodland with a path meandering through them. H and S 18m x 10m (60ft x 30ft). CO south-west China to Nepal

### Cupressus sempervirens 'Pyramidalis' (syn. 'Stricta')

This very dense, narrow conifer has strictly ascending branches that are closely packed with dark green leaves. It gives a strong vertical accent which punctuates the landscape, creating an impression even at a distance. H 20m x 3m (65ft x 9m); ultimately 30m (100ft) tall. CO Mediterranean and western Asia

### Eriobotrya japonica

The large, glossy, deeply grooved leaves make this a useful foliage plant which can be grown as a standard or bush, and also makes a good container subject. Only fairly hardy, it is best grown against a warm wall where, after a very hot summer, it may produce strongly fragrant white flowers. H 8m x 8m (24ft x 24ft). CO China and Japan

### Eucalyptus parviflora

A handsome, slow-growing, evergreen tree that can be pruned to a height of 2m (6ft), making it ideal where space is limited. It has flaking grey bark and narrow blue-green leaves. A very hardy species, unusual among eucalyptus in being tolerant of chalky soils. Grow as a single stem or bush. H and S 15m x 10m (50ft x 30ft). CO Australia

### Pinus banksiana, Pinus mugo, Pinus pinea

*P. banksiana.* This is a gnarled and twisted pine with crooked branches and uneven-size cones. It will grow on most soils but it really thrives in a moist situation. It is very hardy and wind resistant. H and S 10–20m x 3–5m (30–65ft x 9–15ft). CO northern United States, Canada
*P. mugo.* A sprawling pine with many stems that hug the ground before turning upwards. This undemanding tree will grow well in most situations, being very hardy and tolerant of

a wide range of soils. H and S 3.5m x 5m (11ft x 15ft). CO Europe
*P. pinea.* This pine has a dense, umbrella-shaped canopy of thin, grey-green needles above a clear stem of deeply fissured, grey-black bark. The trunk often leans, and the overall effect is gnarled and characterful. The tree does well in sandy soils and maritime regions. H and S 10m–15m x 10m (30ft–50ft x 30ft). CO Mediterranean

### Quercus ilex

This evergreen oak can be grown as a standard with a dense crown of small, leathery, dark green leaves, as these lend themselves well to clipping. This tree thrives in all well-drained soils, and is particularly well suited to maritime areas, where it can be grown to form a large, rigid hedge or a screen. H and S 25m x 20m (80ft x 65ft). CO Mediterranean and south-western Europe

### Trachycarpus fortunei

A striking palm with a tall single trunk clothed with the shaggy, fibrous remains of the old leaf bases. The huge fan-shaped leaves are borne on long, stout stems from the top of the trunk and live for many years. Hardy in the warmer counties if given a sheltered position away from strong winds. H and S 4m x 3m (12ft x 9ft). CO central China

# Materials

All the elements of a minimalist garden need to contribute to the overall composition. The quality of materials and their relationship with each other are crucial in this context. Ornamentation is inappropriate. Natural materials are the preferred choice as they improve with weathering, and have the added ingredient of subtle tones and textures.

There are two golden rules to follow. First, consider whether the local material may be a suitable option as, connected to the ambient light and atmosphere, they can give a garden its special regional character. Secondly, it is very important to understand the properties of the materials and then to work with them. A soft, mellow limestone may be perfect for constructing random, dry-stone walling, but may be too soft for paving, where it might be susceptible to frost. Minimalism involves expressing materials to their potential, and must include a careful study of how they are best cut, jointed, and how they will weather.

STONE There is such an enormous range, from black volcanic rock to white limestone, and a variety of textures in between. It can be used as a background material, such as smooth paving or can be hand crafted as a focal piece of sculpture. Although expensive, it can also be used in the lower budget garden as crushed stone or stone chippings, which suit the contemporary garden style, and allow planting to be grown through.

▶ Cubes of granite setts are used as a separating band between grass and gravel. The setts are excellent for this situation, as their small module (100 x 100 x 100mm or 4 x 4 x 4in) allows the frequent joints to define a curve.

▲ Beach pebbles form a textured background for the reflecting pool, which in turn echoes the glass panel alongside. The mirroring properties of the water duplicate the display of antique olive pots on the giant rendered steps.

▼ A composition that blends different materials, all precisely finished. The painted mild steel column structure supports toughened glass panels on bright stainless steel fittings. The floor is sawn limestone (whit-bed Portland stone) and the coloured panels are made of Italian polished plaster.

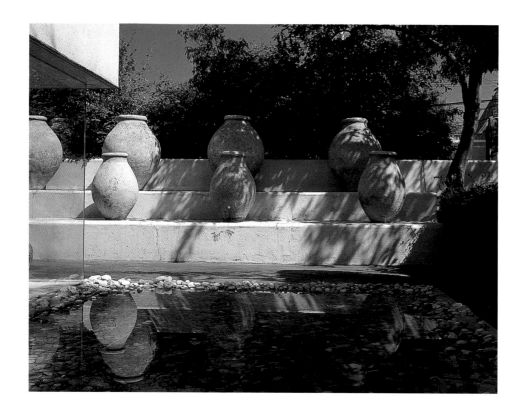

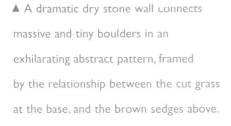

▲ A dramatic dry stone wall connects massive and tiny boulders in an exhilarating abstract pattern, framed by the relationship between the cut grass at the base, and the brown sedges above.

◀ These curved planks demonstrate the versatility of wood, which can be bent to follow the shape of a subframe. The upside-down hull profile catches the light at the top and blends beautifully with the stone chippings at the base.

WOOD This offers a range of types, colours and textures and is cheaper to buy than stone, although it is not last as longlasting. Nevertheless, its warmth and approachability bring a friendly note into garden design. It is ideal for fencing, paving (as decking), garden structures and furniture. It can be purchased pre-treated against rot, it can be oiled or varnished, it can be painted or it can be left unstained to weather to a silver patina. For decking, western red cedar is light, durable and attractive, whereas oak is excellent for supporting structures. Both weather to a beautiful silver within six months. Although exotic hardwoods are hardwearing, check that they are from a sustainable resource.

SMALL MODULE MATERIALS Bricks can be used equally well for paving, walling and retaining structures. For the minimalist garden, special attention must be paid to their detailed design. Handmade bricks, which weather the best, will be made with a tolerance of sizes and so great skill is required to create a precise, rather than a romantic look. Granite setts can be similarly rewarding if the design and craftsmanship is up to standard.

OTHER MATERIALS Non traditional materials can provide the precision required for the minimalist style. Glass and steel can be combined to give height and a vertical dimension, as well as unique reflective properties. High strength, soil resistant fabrics can provide shelter, and a feeling of lightness and movement to an otherwise static scene.

# Index

Page numbers in italics refer to picture captions

## Authors Acknowledgments

There is not the space, especially within a book on minimalism, to be able credit fully the very many people who have helped to make this book possible. But for their support and encouragement, my sincere thanks go to all the team at Mitchell Beazley, who have at all times worked professionally and unstintingly in their efforts to produce a book of the highest standards. Also, to all the designers, garden makers and owners, for giving their time and knowledge and whose work is a

wonderful inspiration. My grateful personal thanks to those who have helped me, including my wife, Kathryn, for her great support, insight and expertise, Georgina Capel, Katie Guillebaud (for her inspired contribution to the plant directory), Casey Horton, and to my clients, for allowing me to design their projects in the first place, and then for their patience during those periods while I have been absent without leave working on the manuscript.

## Photographic Acknowledgments

The publishers would like to thank the following for their kind permission to reproduce the photographs in this book.

KEY TO ABBREVIATIONS

**A** Arcaid **AC** Andres Casillas **AL** Andrew Lawson **BGCL** Berry's Garden Company, London **CBH** Christopher Bradley-Hole **CJ** Charles Jencks **CM** Cesar Manrique **CNGP** Clive Nichols Garden Pictures **CP** Camera Press **DC** David Chipperfield **DG** Dennis Gilbert **DS** David Spero **FS** Fritz von der Schulenberg **GGS** Georgia Glynn-Smith **GM** Glenn Murcutt **GMa** Garden Matters **GPL** The Garden Picture Library **HF** Helen Fickling **HF/TB** Hudson Featherstone/Tim Brotherton **HP** Hugh Palmer **HY** Herbert Ypama **IA** The Interior Archive **JG** John Glover **JH** Jerry Harpur **JP** Jerry Pavia **JPa** John Pawson **JS** Javier Sordo **JY** Jose Yturbe **MH** Marijke Heuff **MM** Marianne Majerus **MMa** Mitsuo Matsuoka **MS** Martha Schwartz **NK** Nicholas Kane **NTPL** National Trust Photographic Library **OP** Octopus Publishing Group Ltd **OVS** Oehme and Van Sweden, Washington, D.C. **PS** Pawson Silvestrin **RB** Richard Bryant **RG** Richard Glover **RM** Rick Mather **RS** Ron Sutherland **SIA** Sven-Ingvar Andersson **TA** Tadao Ando Architect and Associates **TH** Tim Harvey **V** View **VS** Vladimir Sitta

l left r right c centre t top b bottom

1 GPL/Lamontagne; 2–3 TA/MMa; 4–5 IA/HY/architect: AC; 6–7 RG/architect: John Pawson; 7tl A/RB/Hancock Shaker Village, Mass., USA; 8tl A/Bill Tingey; 8br Christie's Images; 9 Wagamama Limited; 10t OP; 10b Norstaal/Ottar Uthaug; 11 Vitra Design Museum; 12 IA/HY; 15t Bridgeman Art Library/Noortman (London) Ltd; 15b V/Peter Cook/architect: Mies van der Rohe; 16l VS/Terragram Pty. Ltd; 16r VS/Terragram Pty. Ltd; 16–17 Belle/Simon Kenny/designer: VS; 18 A/Reiner Blunck/architect: GM; 19 A/Reinner Blunck/architect: GM; 20 GPL/Ron Sutherland/designer: Paul Fleming Design, Australia; 22 V/DG/architect: Sanya Polescuk; 23l Sanya Polescuk; 23br V/DG/architect: Sanya Polescuk; 24 RG/ architect: JPa; 25 IA/Tim Beddow/architect: JPa; 26tr MM/designer: Stephen Woodhams; 26bl GPL/JG/designer: Dan Pearson; 27 IA/FS/architect: Nico Rensch; 28 V/DG/architect: RM; 29 V/DG/architect: RM; 31 V/Chris Gascoigne/architect: Stanton Williams; 32–33 V/Chris Gascoigne/architect: Stanton Williams; 34 A/John Edward Linden/designer: Christopher Mazeika; 36tl Mark Guard; 36–37 A/John Edward Linden/designer: Christopher Mazeika; 38–39 A/RB/architect: DC; 40–41 A/RB/architect: DC; 41tr A/RB/architect: DC; 41br A/RB/architect: DC; 42 A/RB/architect: Mark Guard; 44 Tim Street–Porter/architect: Luis Barragan; 45 HP; 46l SIA; 46–47 MH/Rosendal Exhibition, Stockholm 1998/designer: SIA; 48–49 MH/Rosendal Exhibition, Stockholm 1998/designer: SIA; 49r MH/Rosendal Exhibition, Stockholm 1998/designer: SIA; 50 IA/HY/architect: JY; 51 IA/HY/architect: JY; 52tl IA/HY/architect: JY; 52–53 IA/HY/architect: JY; 54l MS/TH/designer: MS Inc.; 54r MS Inc.; 55 MS/TH/designer: MS Inc.; 56tl MS/THy/designer: MS Inc.; 57 MS/TH/designer: MS Inc.; 58l GPL/JP; 58–59 GPL/JP; 60t VS; 60b VS/Terragram Pty. Ltd; 61 VS/Terragram Pty. Ltd; 62–63 IA/Cecilia Innes/architect: JY; 64–65 AL/designer: CBH; 65br CBH; 66 AL/designer: CBH; 67tl AL/designer: CBH; 67br AL/designer: CBH; 68 CNGP/designer: CBH; 69 AL/designer: CBH; 70–71 IA/HY/architect: AC; 71br IA/HY/architect: AC; 72–73 IA/HY/architect: AC; 74 IA/HY/architect: AC; 75 IA/HY/architect: AC; 76–77 Howard Sooley © Vogue/The Conde Nast Publications Ltd/Charles Worthington; 78l TA/MMa/ architect: TA; 78r TA; 79 TA/TA/architect: TA; 80–81 A/RB/architect: TA; 82 A/RB/architect: SS; 83 DS/architect: SS; 84l SS; 84–85 DS/architect: SS; 86–87 DS/architect: SS; 88 SS 88–89 SS/architect: SS; 90–91 CP/Kurtz; 92–93 Elizabeth Whiting & Associates; 92b A/Ken Kirkwood/architect: Norman Foster Associates; 93b V/Peter Cook/architect: Richard Rogers Partnership; 94 TA/TA architect: TA 95t TA/Hiroshi Kobayashi/architect: TA; 95b /TA; 96l GPL/GGS/architect: RM; 96–97 GPL/GGS/architect: RM; 98 JH/designer: Edwina von Gal; 99 JH/designer: Edwina von Gal; 100 JH/design: BGCL; 101 JH/design: BGCL; 102–103 JH/design: BGCL; 104bl JH/designer: TD; 104–105 JH/designer: TD; 106–107 JH/designer: TD; 108l OP/designer: CBH; 108–109 OP/NK/designer: CBH; 110–111 OP/NK/designer: CBH; 111t CBH; 111b OP/NK/designer: CBH; 112 IA/HY; 114t HP; 114b Hockney/'A Bigger Splash' 1967, acrylic on canvas (96"x96") © David Hockney; 115t A/Scott Frances/architect: Frank Lloyd Wright; 115b VS/Terragram Pty. Ltd; 116 TA/TA/architect: TA 117t TA/Shigeo Ogawa/architect: TA; 117bl TA/TA/ architect: TA; 117br TA; 118 V/Peter Cook/architect: Julian Powell Tuck; 120 GPL/RS/architect: Duane Paul Design Team; 121 GPL/RS/architect: Duane Paul Design Team; 122 JH/designers: OVS; 123r JH/designers: OVS; 124 JH/designers: OVS; 125 JH/designers: OVS; 126 IA/HY/architect: JS; 127 IA/HY/architect: JS; 128–129 IA/HY/architect: JS; 130 A/RB/architects: PS; 131 A/RB/architects: PS; 132–133 A/RB/architects: PS; 133r JPa; 134–135 HF/TB; 136 HF/TB; 137tl HF/TB; 137br HF/TB; 138l HF/ 138–139 HF/TB; 140bl IA/HY/architect: JS; 140r CNGP/Preen Manor, Shropshire; 141 GPL/RS; 142–143 GPL/Steven Wooster/designer: Ted Smyth; 144 GMa/designer: Derek Jarman; 146–147 IA/FS; 146b CNGP/Chenies Manor, Bucks; 147b HP; 148–149 GPL/Howard Rice; 150 IA/FS/designers: Arabella Lennox-Boyd/John Stefanidis; 151 IA/FS/ designers: Arabella Lennox-Boyd/John Stafanidis; 152l MH/Madame N. de Vesian, France; 152–153 MH/Madame N. de Vesian, France; 154–155 MH/Castle and Gardens, Gourdon, France; 155r MH/Castle and Gardens, Gourdon, France; 156 CNGP/designer: CM; 157 CNGP/designer: CM; 158–159 CNGP/designer: CM; 160 JH/designers: OVS; 161 JH/designers: OVS; 162tl JH/designers: OVS; 162bl JH/designers: OVS; 162–163 JH/designers: OVS; 164 GMa/John Fowler; 166–167 NTPL/Stephen Robson; 166b NTPL/Ian Shaw; 167b MS/Dartington Hall, Devon; 168l MS/designer: MS Inc.; 168–169 MS/designer: MS Inc.; 170 CNGP/designer: Gun Lindblad; 171t IA/Helen Fickling; 171b CNGP/designer: Julie Toll; 172 GMa/ John Feltwell/Parc André Citroën, France; 173t GMa/John Feltwell/Parc André Citroën, France; 173b IA/HF/Parc André Citroën, France; 174 IA/HF; 175 IA/HF; 176–177t MS/designer: MS Inc.; 176b MS Inc.; 177r MS/Marc Treib/designer: MS; 178tl GMa; 178bl CNGP/Hannah Peschar Gallery; 178–179 IA/C. Simon Sykes; 180–181 MM/designer: CJ; 182–183 MM/designer: CJ; 183tr MM/designer: CJ; 183br MM/designer: CJ; 184l Janis Hall; 184–185 Janis Hall/designer: Janis Hall; 186–187 GPL/JP; 188 MM/designer: Jacques Wirtz; 189tl GPL/MH/designer: Ton Ter Linden; 189tr AL/Munich Westpark, Germany, 189b NTPL/Stephen Robson; 190 GPL/MH; 191l GPL/Linda Burgess; 191c GPL/JP; 191r GPL/Michel Viard; 192l GPL/MH; 192c GPL/RS; 192r GPL/Jacqui Hurst; 193l GPL/Didier Willery; 193c GPL/JG; 193r GPL/Mayer/Le Scanff; 194l GPL/JP; 194c GPL/JS Sira; 194r GPL/JP; 195l GPL/Howard Rice; 195c GPL/JS Sira; 195r GPL/MH; 196l GPL/JP; 196c GPL/JG; 196r GPL/Eric Cron; 197l GPL/JG; 197c GPL/JS Sira; 197r GPL/Brigitte Thomas; 198l Mitchell Beazley/NK; 198c GPL/ MH; 198r GPL/JS Sira; 199l GPL/JG; 199c GPL/JG; 199r GPL/Christies Carter; 200l GPL/Sunniva Harte; 200c GPL/Linda Burgess; 200r GPL/Sunniva Harte; 201l GPL/Didier Willery 201c GPL/Brigitte Thomas; 201r GPL/JG; 202l IA/HY; 202r CBH/designer: CBH; 203tl GPL; 203bl MM/designer: Jacques Wirtz; 203r GPL/Erika Craddock/designer: VS.

The Publishers also wish to thank Arlene Sobel for her editorial help.